SELECTIONS

FROM

BROWNING'S POEMS

EDITED BY

J. CHARLES HAZZARD, Ph.D.

STATE NORMAL COLLEGE
NATCHITOCHES, LOUISIANA

—◦◦◦◦—

ALLYN AND BACON

BOSTON   NEW YORK   CHICAGO
ATLANTA   SAN FRANCISCO

IAI

Norwood Press
J. S. Cushing Co. — Berwick & Smith Co.
Norwood, Mass., U.S.A.

PREFACE

THIS collection of the poems of Browning was prepared for high-school students. It is intended to serve as an introduction to the poetry of one whose poems present difficulties even to scholars. Simplicity has therefore been the guiding principle in the selection, the arrangement, and the editing of the poems.

This edition includes all the poems which are on the list of the College Entrance Requirements. The order of arrangement is that which Browning himself preferred in the selection of his poems which he made and published before his death.

The notes are purposely made complete and simple, for there is much in Browning which requires interpretation, even to pupils of good literary training.

It is the hope of the editor that the book will be the means of interesting students in the poetry of "the manliest, the strongest, the lifefulest, the deepest and the thoughtfulest poet, the one most needing earnest study, and the most worthy of it." If such be the case, the book will not have been written in vain.

J. C. H.

FEBRUARY, 1921.

CONTENTS

Contents

INTRODUCTION

BROWNING'S LIFE

ROBERT BROWNING, the third of that name, was born in Camberwell, a suburb of London, May 7, 1812. He was the eldest of three children. Robert Browning's father, when a young man, had been sent by his father to the West Indies, where he held a lucrative position on a sugar plantation. But on account of his objections to slavery, he gave up his place and returned to England, where he became an official in the Bank of England.

Although the elder Browning was a successful business man, his tastes were æsthetic and literary, and his leisure was devoted to the study of classical and modern literatures. He also had considerable skill as an artist, for he drew vigorous pictures and caricatures of the patrons of the Bank whom he was supposed to serve. According to the statement of his son, he was also a skilled versifier. As the father's position gave him a competence, he generously permitted his son to choose his life work without regard to financial returns. "He secured for me," says the poet, "all the ease and comfort that a literary man needs to do good work."

The poet's mother was Sarah Anne Wiedemann, the daughter of a German ship owner settled in Dundee, Scotland. She was possessed of a deep piety and an artistic nature. "She was," says Carlyle, "the true type of a Scottish gentlewoman." The relation between mother and son was unusually close. "A divine woman," he called her, and at her death in 1849 he gave way for a time to overwhelming sorrow.

For the most part Browning's education was received at home. Camberwell at that time was still rural enough to permit him to wander about through woods and open country. Here he learned to know nature, and early developed that keen faculty of observation which characterized him throughout his whole life. His love for wild animals he seems to have inherited from his mother, who encouraged him in his collecting, and he was constantly bringing home pets of all sorts.

After he was ten years old he spent some time at a private school in the neighborhood. When he was fourteen, he first became acquainted with the poems of Shelley and Keats. He tells us how he read these poets to the accompaniment of two nightingales in the trees of his father's garden. From that time he felt himself consecrated to the high task of writing poetry. He began to prepare himself for the work by "sedulous cultivation of the powers of his mind" by study at home, and by travel abroad.

For the next four years Browning had private tutors at home. He studied music under various masters. To strengthen his body he took lessons in dancing, riding, boxing, and fencing. He kept up his work in art and trained himself further by frequent visits to the museums. At eighteen he was matriculated at the University of London where he studied for two years.

In January, 1833, Browning published his first poem *Pauline*, anonymously. In it we find many echoes of

Shelley, especially of *Alastor*. To certain critics the work made a strong appeal, for in spite of its crudities they recognized in it the promise of genius. The publication of this poem was followed by a period of travel in Russia. In 1835 Browning published *Paracelsus*, the first poem to which he attached his name. This is a study of the life of the early Renaissance alchemist, mystic, and physician Paracelsus. Although the work was coolly received and added nothing to Browning's popularity, his genius was admitted by a group of critics, and he was received into the foremost literary circles of London. This was the means of making him acquainted with such men as Macready, the actor, Dickens, Talfourd, Leigh Hunt, Barry Cornwall, Wordsworth, and Landor.

On one occasion Macready proposed that Browning write a play for him. Browning complied with the request and produced the play *Strafford*, a drama founded on the tragic career of Thomas Wentworth, the Earl of Strafford, the minister of Charles I. The play was produced at Covent Garden Theater in 1837. After a brief run it was withdrawn.

Browning turned his attention next to the completion of a long poem *Sordello* on which he had been working for some time and which he had laid aside for the drama. In 1838 he visited Italy that he might see for himself the scenes he was describing in his poem. "Italy was my university," he was accustomed to say. In 1840 *Sordello* was published. It did not add to Browning's reputation. In fact its effect upon his fame as a poet was disastrous. Many stories are told of the difficulties of various persons in trying to read it. The publication of this poem, so obscure in parts, marks the beginning of

what Browning called the period of "prolonged deso-
lateness," when for twenty years his poems met with almost complete indifference in the land of his birth.

From 1841 to 1846 he published a series of poems to
which he gave the somewhat fantastic name of "*Bells
and Pomegranates*," a title suggested by a verse in Exodus.
By this name he intended to indicate "a mixture of music
with discoursing, sound with sense, poetry with thought."
Under this title he brought out eight numbers, including *Pippa Passes*, 1841, *Dramatic Lyrics*, 1842, *Dramatic
Romances and Lyrics*, 1845, and several of the dramas.

Of Browning's dramas it must be said that they never
have and probably never will achieve popularity as act-
ing plays. They are too subjective, too analytic. "His
genius, bent as it was on the interpretation of spiritual
phenomena, could ill brook the demands of the acted
drama that all this interpretation should stop with visible,
intelligible, and satisfactory action, capable of histrionic
expression. Browning's eager penetration of the arcana
of life was too absorbing to permit him to call a halt when
the actor on the stage could go no farther."

At this time began Browning's courtship of Elizabeth
Barrett, whose works were beginning to be read widely.
In 1844 she had published a volume of poems which
Browning admired greatly. He wrote to her, expressing his appreciation of her work and asking permission to
call. As Miss Barrett was an invalid, having injured her
back by a fall from a horse, she at first refused to see
him. But later through the efforts of John Kenyon
the two were brought together.

Almost immediately Browning made her an offer of
marriage, which she at first declined on account of her

poor health. But Browning's masterful wooing was at length rewarded and she consented to marry him. As her father opposed her marrying at all, she and Browning were secretly married on September 12, 1846, at Marylebone Church, London. A week after their secret marriage they started for Italy. Mrs. Browning made many vain efforts to placate her obdurate father. He refused to see her again and returned her letters unopened. This wounded her deeply, for she had devotedly loved him.

Journeying by slow stages, the Brownings reached Florence in April, 1847. In 1848 they found what was to be their permanent home, the second floor of the Casa Guidi, a shrine ever since consecrated to their memory. Here they lived quietly and worked industriously. Both of them became intensely interested in the efforts that were being made by patriotic Italians to free their native land, an interest frequently reflected in the poems of both poets.

On March 9, 1849, their son Wiedemann, later known as "Penini" or "Pen" Browning, was born. At about this time Browning's mother died. He was a long time in recovering from the loss. "He had loved his mother," wrote Mrs. Browning, "as such passionate natures can love, and I never saw a man so bowed down in an extremity of sorrow — never."

During this long period of his life in Italy Browning produced little; especially is this statement true if we compare the output with his work during the richly productive period from 1841 to 1846. In 1850 he published *Christmas Eve and Easter Day*, a long poem in two parts, in which he treats of the arguments for Christianity, and, five years later, in 1855, *Men and Women*, a collec-

tion of fifty-one poems, a group which has been called
the flower of his genius. "But though the record is
meager as to quantity, lovers of Browning's poetry would
be likely to regard this as not only a central period,
chronologically, but the period when he reached his
highest expression."

It is in this collection that he brought to perfection a
form of poetry which he uses more uniquely than does
any other poet, the dramatic monologue. This type
has the advantage of a dramatic effect without the dramatic form. There is only one speaker, but the effect
of the speech upon implied listeners is clearly brought
out. By this means the dramatic effect is obtained.
Noteworthy also is the great range of these poems. In
them we find represented all the varied aspects of Flor-
entine life.

On June 28, 1861, Mrs. Browning died. Until within
the last few years before her death her health had greatly
improved, and in addition to enjoying the social life of
the city in a limited degree, she was able to publish poems
that attracted more general notice than did the poems of
her husband. In 1851 she published *Casa Guidi Win-
dows*, a collection of poems, and in 1857 her long novel
in verse, *Aurora Leigh*. Although her strength had
been failing for some time, her death was unexpected
and was a great blow to her loving husband. It brought
to a close the beautiful and romantic life they had been
living in Florence and probably affected greatly the
remainder of Browning's career.

Almost immediately he left Italy for England and made
his home in London in a house in Warwick Crescent.
At first he gave himself up to his sorrow, living a life of

loneliness. In 1863 he published a new and complete
collection of his poetical works in three volumes. In
1864 appeared a collection called *Dramatis Personae*,
containing some of his greater poems, such as Rabbi Ben
Ezra, A Death in the Desert, and Abt Vogler. A recog-
nition of his growing fame is seen in the demand for
selections from his work and also in the conferring of
an honorary degree of M. A. by the University of Oxford in 1867. Not long afterwards he was made an
honorary fellow of Balliol College. The University of
Cambridge conferred upon him the degree of Doctor of
Civil Law in 1879 and the University of Oxford gave him
the same degree in 1882.

In 1863 he suddenly changed his habits and began to
accept invitations, entering again into the social life of
London. After the death of his father in 1866, he and
his sister Sarianna, who had become his constant com-
panion, lived together in London, although they frequently passed their summers in Brittany, Wales, and
Scotland. Later he took his sister to Italy, although he
always avoided Florence.

In 1868 and 1869 Browning published a long work in
four volumes called *The Ring and the Book*. This he
destined to be his *magnum opus* and on it he had labored
for many years. During his residence in Florence he
had picked up at a book-stall an "old yellow Book"
which contained an account of a tragic story of the seven-
teenth century. This story he brooded over until he had
seen it in all its relations to humanity. The poem has a
novel structure. In it the story of the forced marriage
of the young girl Pompilia to the Count Guido, her
rescue from his clutches by the Canon Caponsacchi,

her murder, the trial of the Count, the arguments of the lawyers, and the review of the case by the Pope who judged it, all are given. The story is retold ten times from all different viewpoints. It is a series of dramatic monologues, enlarged to fit the occasion.

In her commentary on Browning's works Mrs. Orr traces the influence of Mrs. Browning in the character of Pompilia. This work Browning seems to have intended to be a monument to the memory of his dead wife, consecrated to her whom he always regarded as the superior poetical genius and whose works he was never tired of praising. "The simple truth is," he wrote to a friend, "that she was the poet and I the clever person by comparison: remember her limited experience of all kinds, and what she made of it. Remember, on the other hand, how my uninterrupted health and strength and practice with the world have helped me."

In 1871 he published *Balaustion's Adventure*, in 1875 *Aristophanes' Apology*, and in 1877 his translation of *The Agamemnon of Aeschylus*. This group of poems represents Browning's criticism of Greek art and thought. They are the fruits of his prolonged study of Greek poetry, especially of the Greek dramatists. During these years, when fame had come to him, and he had been honored during his lifetime beyond any other English poet by having a society formed to study and interpret his works, Browning led a semi-public life.

As his biographer Sharp states: "Everybody wished him to come and dine; and he did his utmost to gratify everybody. He saw everything; read all the notable books; kept himself acquainted with the leading contents of the journals and magazines; conducted a large correspondence; read new French, German, and Italian books of mark; read and translated Euripides and Aeschylus; knew all the gossip of the literary clubs, salons, and the studios; was a frequenter of afternoon tea-parties; and then, over and above it, he was Browning: the most profoundly subtle mind that has exercised itself in poetry since Shakespeare."

Browning's later works, with the exception, perhaps, of the *Dramatic Idyls*, added but little to his reputation. He published *The Red Cotton Night-Cap Country* in 1873 and *The Inn Album* in 1875. These are long narrative poems. The next collection of his poems *Pacchiarotto* is marked by obscurities and oddities. *The Dramatic Idyls*, 1879, 1880, however, contain some excellent work.

Browning's visits to Italy now became more frequent. Still he avoided Florence on account of the sad memories associated with that city. He revisited Asolo, where he had laid the scene of *Pippa Passes* in his earlier days, and here he gathered the last collection of his poems, to which he gave the name of *Asolando*. Browning's son had married and had taken up his permanent residence at Venice and had bought the old Palazzo Rezzonica. Here Browning came and after a brief illness died suddenly on December 12, 1889. By a coincidence *Asolando* was published in London on the same day. Browning was buried in the Poets' Corner of Westminster Abbey on the last day of the year. As a mark of respect to his memory the Italian government placed a tablet on the wall of the Palazzo Rezzonica with a suitable inscription which closes with these lines from *De Gustibus*:

> "Open my heart and you will see
> Graved inside of it, 'Italy.'"

BROWNING'S POETRY

One of the most impressive facts in Browning's works is the immense variety of subjects with which he deals. All ages, all varieties of experience, all periods of the world's history are to be found in his pages. Browning takes all human life as his province. He proposes to understand "God and his works and all God's intercourse with the human soul." Nothing in man is too insignificant or too remote to be included in his pages, provided it have its effect on man's soul.

Browning has been called a romanticist by some critics and has been claimed as a realist by the opposite camp. Probably both sides are right within limits, for in the freedom of choice which he displays in selecting his subjects, Browning is clearly romantic, but in his method of treating his chosen subject he is realistic. His choice of subject seems to have been determined by the belief that individual feeling and motive are the only true life. His range of subject covers a great deal that is painful, but nothing that is repulsive. His treatment of his subject is always picturesque. It raises a distinct image of the person or action he intends to describe.

Browning may be regarded as a romanticist on account of his invention or adaptation of a particular form of verse for each occasion. As he believed that every circumstance, every occasion should be expressed by an appropriate metrical form, he is constantly experimenting with new and unusual metrical combinations. In his work the metrical form suggests by its rhythm the underlying idea of the poem, as for example in "How We Brought the Good News from Ghent to Aix," where the rhythm suggests the galloping of horses. His verse is subordinate to his theory of the poetic art. Always it was his principle that sense should not be sacrificed to sound. Thought before expression, matter before form, are marked characteristics of his work. This effort to clothe his subject with a suitable form occasionally led him into obscurity, but in most cases the effort was successful.

Browning's favorite method of treating a subject was to examine it through the eyes of some suitable character whom he selected or invented for the purpose. This involved only a one-sided survey, a survey from only one viewpoint. Sometimes this also causes obscurity, for the reader forgets that the poet is not trying to give a complete account of a certain event but only such a partial one as his assumed character might obtain.

Much has been written about Browning's philosophy of life. Although a complete system of philosophy may be deduced from his works, Browning was concerned rather with man as an individual than with man in the abstract. To him each case was a separate study, for he read the meaning of life and measured its value from the point of view of the individual, not from that of society. Action, energy, daring, persistence are the virtures which he commends for their own sakes, while their opposites he strongly condemns.

But he does not consider this life as final. We are placed here, he thinks, for the purpose of growing enough to enable us to take our part in another life beyond this one. Here we are surrounded by limitations which baffle and retard our growth. Through these limitations come failures, which prevent us from being content with our condition. There is something within us, some divine spark,

which is always spurring us on and urging us to endeavor
to transcend these limitations and reach out for what is
beyond.   But we must find out what these limitations
are and work within them, or life would become nothing
but vain discontent with our condition.   This constant
battle between our aspirations and our limitations makes
up the stress of life.   "Thus, the purpose of life is not
the attainment of any specific end, either selfish or heroic,
but rather the continued progress of the human spirit in
its chosen course."

Browning was an optimist.   He believed that no experience is wasted, that all life is good in its way.   Even
the so-called "evils of life" are not without some good.
If we would remedy them, we need more of the good qual-
ities, the opposite of the evil.   Browning's attitude towards
life cannot be better stated than he himself has expressed
it in one of the stanzas of his last poem, The Epilogue to
Asolando, where he says that he is —

"One who never turned his back but marched breast forward,
   Never doubted clouds would break,
   Never dreamed, tho' right were worsted, wrong would triumph,
   Held we fall to rise, are baffled to fight better,
      Sleep to wake."

BIBLIOGRAPHY

For complete bibliography, see the Bibliography of Biography
and Criticism by J. P. Anderson printed in the *Life of Robert Browning* by William Sharp.

The Complete Works of Robert Browning, 17 vols., ed. A. Birrell and
   F. G. Kenyon.   Smith, Elder & Company.

Complete Works, 12 vols., ed. Charlotte Porter and Helen A. Clarke.

The Complete Poetic and Dramatic Works of Robert Browning, Cambridge Edition, 1 vol., ed. H. E. Scudder.

The Browning Cyclopædia.   Edward Berdoe.

The Poetry of Robert Browning. Stopford Brooke.

An Introduction to the Study of Robert Browning's Poetry. Hiram Corson.

The Life of Robert Browning. Temple Biographies. Reprinted in Everyman's Library. Edward Dowden.

Critical Kit-Kats. Edmund W. Gosse.

Robert Browning. Modern English Writers. C. H. Herford.

Browning as a Philosophical and Religious Teacher. Sir Henry Jones.

A Handbook to the Works of Robert Browning. Mrs. S. Orr.

Life and Letters of Robert Browning. Mrs. S. Orr and Sir F. G. Kenyon.

Browning: How to Know Him. William Lyon Phelps.

Life of Robert Browning. William Sharp. (The standard biography.)

An Introduction to the Study of Browning. Arthur Symons.

The Letters of Robert Browning and Elizabeth Barrett. Two volumes.

CHRONOLOGICAL TABLE

March 6, 1806.	Elizabeth Barrett born at Coxhoe, county of Durham.
May 7, 1812.	Robert Browning born in Camberwell, London.
1825.	Browning read Shelley and Keats.
1826.	Browning left Mr. Ready's school.
1827.	Alfred and Charles Tennyson: *Poems by Two Brothers.*
1830.	Alfred Tennyson: *Poems, chiefly Lyrical.*
1833.	Browning: *Pauline*, published anonymously.
	Tennyson: *Poems.*
1833–1834.	Browning travelled in Russia and Italy.
1835.	Browning: *Paracelsus.*
1837.	Browning: *Strafford.* Acted May 1 at Covent Garden Theater.
1840.	Browning: *Sordello.*
1841.	Browning: *Pippa Passes.*
1842.	Browning: *Dramatic Lyrics.*
	Tennyson: *Poems.*
1843.	Browning: *A Blot in the 'Scutcheon.*
1844.	Elizabeth Barrett: *Poems.*
	Browning: *Colombe's Birthday.*

Jan. 10, 1845.   Correspondence between Robert Browning and Elizabeth Barrett begun.

May 20,   Their first meeting.

     Browning: *Dramatic Romances and Lyrics.*

Sept. 12, 1846.   Robert Browning and Elizabeth Barrett married at Marylebone Church, London.

Oct., 1846 to April, 1847.   In Pisa.

April 20, 1847.   Took up their residence at Florence.

March 9, 1849.   Birth of Wiedemann Browning.

March   Browning's mother died.

     1850.   Elizabeth Barrett Browning: *Sonnets from the Portuguese.*

     1850.   Browning: *Christmas Eve and Easter Day.*

     Tennyson: *In Memoriam.*

     1851.   Elizabeth Barrett Browning: *Casa Guidi Windows.*

     1855.   Browning: *Men and Women.*

     1857.   Elizabeth Barrett Browning: *Aurora Leigh.*

June   1860.   Browning found the "Yellow Book."

June 29, 1861.   Elizabeth Barrett Browning died.

July   Browning left Florence and resided in London.

     1864.   Browning: *Dramatis Personae.*

     1868.   Browning: *The Ring and the Book,* finished 1869.

     1871.   Browning: *Balaustion's Adventure.*

     Browning: *Prince Hohenstiel-Schwangau.*

     1872.   Browning: *Fifine at the Fair.*

     1873.   Browning: *Red Cotton Night-Cap Country.*

     1875.   Browning: *Aristophanes' Apology.*

     Browning: *The Inn Album.*

     1876.   Browning: *Pacchiarotto and How He Worked in Distemper.*

     1877.   Browning: *The Agamemnon of Aeschylus* translated.

     1878.   Browning: *La Saisiaz; The Two Poets of Croisic.*

     1879.   Browning revisits Italy for the first time after his wife's death.

     Browning: *Dramatic Idyls,* First Series.

     1880.   Browning: *Dramatic Idyls,* Second Series.

     1883.   Browning: *Jocoseria.*

     1884.   Browning: *Ferishtah's Fancies.*

BROWNING'S POEMS

MY STAR

ALL that I know
   Of a certain star
Is, it can throw
   (Like the angled spar)
Now a dart of red,   5
   Now a dart of blue;
Till my friends have said
   They would fain see, too,
My star that dartles the red and the blue!
Then it stops like a bird; like a flower, hangs furled: 10
   They must solace themselves with the Saturn above it.
What matter to me if their star is a world?
   Mine has opened its soul to me; therefore I love it.

A FACE

IF one could have that little head of hers
   Painted upon a background of pale gold,
Such as the Tuscan's early art prefers!
   No shade encroaching on the matchless mould
Of those two lips, which should be opening soft   5
   In the pure profile; not as when she laughs,
For that spoils all: but rather as if aloft
   Yon hyacinth, she loves so, leaned its staff's
Burthen of honey-coloured buds to kiss
And capture 'twixt the lips apart for this.   10

I

Then her lithe neck, three fingers might surround,
How it should waver on the pale gold ground
Up to the fruit-shaped, perfect chin it lifts!
I know, Correggio loves to mass, in rifts
Of heaven, his angel faces, orb on orb   15
Breaking its outline, burning shades absorb:
But these are only massed there, I should think,
   Waiting to see some wonder momently
   Grow out, stand full, fade slow against the sky
   (That's the pale ground you'd see this sweet face by),   20
   All heaven, meanwhile, condensed into one eye
Which fears to lose the wonder, should it wink.

MY LAST DUCHESS

FERRARA

THAT's my last Duchess painted on the wall,
Looking as if she were alive.   I call
That piece a wonder, now: Frà Pandolf's hands
Worked busily a day, and there she stands.
Will't please you sit and look at her? I said   5
" Frà Pandolf " by design, for never read
Strangers like you that pictured countenance,
The depth and passion of its earnest glance,
But to myself they turned (since none puts by
The curtain I have drawn for you, but I)   10
And seemed as they would ask me, if they durst,
How such a glance came there; so, not the first
Are you to turn and ask thus.   Sir, 'twas not
Her husband's presence only, called that spot
Of joy into the Duchess' cheek: perhaps   15
Frà Pandolf chanced to say " Her mantle laps

Over my lady's wrist too much," or " Paint
Must never hope to reproduce the faint
Half-flush that dies along her throat: " such stuff
Was courtesy, she thought, and cause enough   20
For calling up that spot of joy. She had
A heart — how shall I say? — too soon made glad,
Too easily impressed; she liked whate'er
She looked on, and her looks went everywhere.
Sir, 'twas all one! My favour at her breast,   25
The dropping of the daylight in the West,
The bough of cherries some officious fool
Broke in the orchard for her, the white mule
She rode with round the terrace — all and each
Would draw from her alike the approving speech,   30
Or blush, at least. She thanked men, — good! but thanked
Somehow — I know not how — as if she ranked
My gift of a nine-hundred-years-old name
With anybody's gift. Who'd stoop to blame
This sort of trifling? Even had you skill   35
In speech — (which I have not) — to make your will
Quite clear to such an one, and say, " Just this
Or that in you disgusts me; here you miss,
Or there exceed the mark " — and if she let
Herself be lessoned so, nor plainly set   40
Her wits to yours, forsooth, and made excuse,
— E'en then would be some stooping; and I choose
Never to stoop. Oh sir, she smiled, no doubt,
Whene'er I passed her; but who passed without
Much the same smile? This grew; I gave commands;   45
Then all smiles stopped together. There she stands
As if alive. Will't please you rise? We'll meet
The company below, then. I repeat,

The Count your master's known munificence
Is ample warrant that no just pretence   50
Of mine for dowry will be disallowed;
Though his fair daughter's self, as I avowed
At starting, is my object.   Nay, we'll go
Together down, sir.   Notice Neptune, though,
Taming a sea-horse, thought a rarity,   55
Which Claus of Innsbruck cast in bronze for me!

SONGS FROM PIPPA PASSES

I

THE year's at the spring
And day's at the morn;
Morning's at seven;
The hill-side's dew-pearled;
The lark's on the wing;   5
The snail's on the thorn:
God's in his heaven —
All's right with the world!

II

Give her but a least excuse to love me!
When — where —   10
How — can this arm establish her above me,
If fortune fixed her as my lady there,
There already, to eternally reprove me?
(" Hist!" — said Kate the Queen;
But " Oh!" — cried the maiden, binding her tresses, 15
" 'Tis only a page that carols unseen,
Crumbling your hounds their messes!")

Is she wronged? — To the rescue of her honour,
My heart!
Is she poor? — What costs it to be styled a donor?   20
Merely an earth to cleave, a sea to part.
But that fortune should have thrust all this upon her!
(" Nay, list!" — bade Kate the Queen;
And still cried the maiden, binding her tresses,
" 'Tis only a page that carols unseen   25
Fitting your hawks their jesses!")

III

You'll love me yet! — and I can tarry
    Your love's protracted growing:
June reared that bunch of flowers you carry,
    From seeds of April's sowing.   30

I plant a heartful now: some seed
    At least is sure to strike.
And yield — what you'll not pluck indeed,
    Not love, but, may be, like.

You'll look at least on love's remains,   35
    A grave's one violet:
Your look? — that pays a thousand pains.
    What's death?   You'll love me yet!

EURYDICE TO ORPHEUS

A PICTURE BY LEIGHTON

But give them me, the mouth, the eyes, the brow!
Let them once more absorb me!   One look now
    Will lap me round forever, not to pass
Out of its light, though darkness lie beyond:

Hold me but safe again within the bond   5
  Of one immortal look!   All woe that was,
Forgotten, and all terror that may be,
Defied, — no past is mine, no future: look at me!

"THE MOTH'S KISS, FIRST!"

THE moth's kiss, first!
Kiss me as if you made believe
You were not sure, this eve,
How my face, your flower, had pursed
Its petals up; so, here and there   5
You brush it, till I grow aware
Who wants me, and wide ope I burst.

The bee's kiss, now!
Kiss me as if you entered gay
My heart at some noonday,   10
A bud that dares not disallow
The claim, so all is rendered up,
And passively its shattered cup
Over your head to sleep I bow.

MEETING AT NIGHT

THE gray sea and the long black land;
And the yellow half-moon large and low;
And the startled little waves that leap
In fiery ringlets from their sleep,
As I gain the cove with pushing prow,   5
And quench its speed i' the slushy sand.

Then a mile of warm sea-scented beach;
Three fields to cross till a farm appears;
A tap at the pane, the quick sharp scratch
And blue spurt of a lighted match, 10
And a voice less loud, thro' its joys and fears,
Than the two hearts beating each to each!

PARTING AT MORNING

ROUND the cape of a sudden came the sea,
And the sun looked over the mountain's rim;
And straight was a path of gold for him, 15
And the need of a world of men for me.

"HOW THEY BROUGHT THE GOOD NEWS FROM GHENT TO AIX"

I SPRANG to the stirrup, and Joris, and he;
I galloped, Dirck galloped, we galloped all three;
"Good speed!" cried the watch, as the gatebolts undrew;
"Speed!" echoed the wall to us galloping through;
Behind shut the postern, the lights sank to rest, 5
And into the midnight we galloped abreast.

Not a word to each other; we kept the great pace
Neck by neck, stride by stride, never changing our place;
I turned in my saddle and made its girths tight,
Then shortened each stirrup, and set the pique right, 10
Rebuckled the cheek-strap, chained slacker the bit,
Nor galloped less steadily Roland a whit.

'Twas moonset at starting; but while we drew near
Lokeren, the cocks crew and twilight dawned clear;

At Boom, a great yellow star came out to see;   15
At Düffeld, 'twas morning as plain as could be;
And from Mecheln church-steeple we heard the half-chime,
So, Joris broke silence with, " Yet there is time!"

At Aershot, up leaped of a sudden the sun,
And against him the cattle stood black every one,   20
To stare thro' the mist at us galloping past,
And I saw my stout galloper Roland at last,
With resolute shoulders, each butting away
The haze, as some bluff river headland its spray:

And his low head and crest, just one sharp ear bent back 25
For my voice, and the other pricked out on his track;
And one eye's black intelligence, — ever that glance
O'er its white edge at me, his own master, askance!
And the thick heavy spum-flakes which aye and anon
His fierce lips shook upwards in galloping on.   30

By Hasselt, Dirck groaned; and cried Joris, " Stay spur!
Your Roos galloped bravely, the fault's not in her,
We'll remember at Aix " — for one heard the quick wheeze
Of her chest, saw the stretched neck and staggering knees,
And sunk tail, and horrible heave of the flank,   35
As down on her haunches she shuddered and sank.

So, we were left galloping, Joris and I,
Past Looz and past Tongres, no cloud in the sky;
The broad sun above laughed a pitiless laugh,
'Neath our feet broke the brittle bright stubble like chaff; 40
Till over by Dalhem a dome-spire sprang white,
And " Gallop," gasped Joris, " for Aix is in sight!"

" How they'll greet us!"—and all in a moment his roan
Rolled neck and croup over, lay dead as a stone;
And there was my Roland to bear the whole weight   45
Of the news which alone could save Aix from her fate,
With his nostrils like pits full of blood to the brim,
And with circles of red for his eye-sockets' rim.

Then I cast loose my buffcoat, each holster let fall,
Shook off both my jack-boots, let go belt and all,   50
Stood up in the stirrup, leaned, patted his ear,
Called my Roland his pet-name, my horse without peer;
Clapped my hands, laughed and sang, any noise, bad or
    good,
Till at length into Aix Roland galloped and stood.

And all I remember is—friends flocking round   55
As I sat with his head 'twixt my knees on the ground;
And no voice but was praising this Roland of mine,
As I poured down his throat our last measure of wine,
Which (the burgesses voted by common consent)
Was no more than his due who brought good news from
    Ghent.   60

INCIDENT OF THE FRENCH CAMP

You know, we French stormed Ratisbon:
    A mile or so away,
On a little mound, Napoleon
    Stood on our storming-day;
With neck out-thrust, you fancy how,   5
    Legs wide, arms locked behind,
As if to balance the prone brow
    Oppressive with its mind.

Just as perhaps he mused " My plans
   That soar, to earth may fall,   10
Let once my army-leader Lannes
   Waver at yonder wall,"—
Out 'twixt the battery-smokes there flew
   A rider, bound on bound
Full-galloping; nor bridle drew   15
   Until he reached the mound.

Then off there flung in smiling joy,
   And held himself erect
By just his horse's mane, a boy:
   You hardly could suspect —   20
(So tight he kept his lips compressed,
   Scarce any blood came through)
You looked twice ere you saw his breast
   Was all but shot in two.

" Well," cried he, " Emperor, by God's grace   25
   We've got you Ratisbon !
The Marshal's in the market-place,
   And you'll be there anon
To see your flag-bird flap his vans
   Where I, to heart's desire,   30
Perched him !"   The chief's eye flashed; his plans
   Soared up again like fire.

The chief's eye flashed; but presently
   Softened itself, as sheathes
A film the mother-eagle's eye   35
   When her bruised eaglet breathes;

" You're wounded ! "   " Nay," the soldier's pride
    Touched to the quick, he said :
" I'm killed, Sire ! "   And his chief beside
    Smiling the boy fell dead.   40

THE LOST LEADER

JUST for a handful of silver he left us,
    Just for a riband to stick in his coat —
Found the one gift of which fortune bereft us,
    Lost all the others she lets us devote ;
They, with the gold to give, doled him out silver,   5
    So much was theirs who so little allowed :
How all our copper had gone for his service !
    Rags — were they purple, his heart had been proud !
We that had loved him so, followed him, honoured him,
    Lived in his mild and magnificent eye,   10
Learned his great language, caught his clear accents,
    Made him our pattern to live and to die !
Shakespeare was of us, Milton was for us,
    Burns, Shelley, were with us, — they watch from their
      graves !
He alone breaks from the van and the freemen,   15
    — He alone sinks to the rear and the slaves !

We shall march prospering, — not thro' his presence ;
    Songs may inspirit us, — not from his lyre ;
Deeds will be done, — while he boasts his quiescence,
    Still bidding crouch whom the rest bade aspire :   20
Blot out his name, then, record one lost soul more,
    One task more declined, one more footpath untrod,
One more devils'-triumph and sorrow for angels,
    One wrong more to man, one more insult to God !

Life's night begins: let him never come back to us!   25
   There would be doubt, hesitation and pain,
Forced praise on our part — the glimmer of twilight,
   Never glad confident morning again!
Best fight on well, for we taught him — strike gallantly,
   Menace our heart ere we master his own;   30
Then let him receive the new knowledge and wait us,
   Pardoned in heaven, the first by the throne!

LOVE AMONG THE RUINS

WHERE the quiet-coloured end of evening smiles,
     Miles and miles
On the solitary pastures where our sheep
     Half-asleep
Tinkle homeward thro' the twilight, stray or stop   5
     As they crop —
Was the site once of a city great and gay,
     (So they say)
Of our country's very capital, its prince
     Ages since   10
Held his court in, gathered councils, wielding far
     Peace or war.

Now, — the country does not even boast a tree,
     As you see,
To distinguish slopes of verdure, certain rills   15
     From the hills
Intersect and give a name to, (else they run
     Into one)
Where the domed and daring palace shot its spires
     Up like fires   20

O'er the hundred-gated circuit of a wall
      Bounding all,
Made of marble, men might march on nor be pressed,
      Twelve abreast.

And such plenty and perfection, see, of grass   25
      Never was!
Such a carpet as, this summer-time, o'erspreads
      And embeds
Every vestige of the city, guessed alone,
      Stock or stone —   30
Where a multitude of men breathed joy and woe
      Long ago;
Lust of glory pricked their hearts up, dread of shame
      Struck them tame;
And that glory and that shame alike, the gold   35
      Bought and sold.

Now, — the single little turret that remains
      On the plains,
By the caper overrooted, by the gourd
      Overscored,   40
While the patching houseleek's head of blossom winks
      Through the chinks —
Marks the basement whence a tower in ancient time
      Sprang sublime,
And a burning ring, all round, the chariots traced   45
      As they raced,
And the monarch and his minions and his dames
      Viewed the games.

And I know, while thus the quiet-coloured eve
      Smiles to leave   50

To their folding, all our many-tinkling fleece
        In such peace,
And the slopes and rills in undistinguished gray
        Melt away —
That a girl with eager eyes and yellow hair   55
        Waits me there
In the turret whence the charioteers caught soul
        For the goal,
When the king looked, where she looks now, breath-
   less, dumb
        Till I come.   60

But he looked upon the city, every side,
        Far and wide,
All the mountains topped with temples, all the
   glades'
        Colonnades,
All the causeys, bridges, aqueducts, — and then,   65
        All the men !
When I do come, she will speak not, she will stand,
        Either hand
On my shoulder, give her eyes the first embrace
        Of my face,   70
Ere we rush, ere we extinguish sight and speech
        Each on each.

In one year they sent a million fighters forth
        South and North,
And they built their gods a brazen pillar high   75
        As the sky,
Yet reserved a thousand chariots in full force —
        Gold, of course.

Oh heart! oh blood that freezes, blood that burns!
      Earth's returns   80
For whole centuries of folly, noise and sin!
      Shut them in,
With their triumphs and their glories and the rest!
      Love is best.

HOME-THOUGHTS, FROM ABROAD

OH, to be in England
Now that April's there,
And whoever wakes in England
Sees, some morning, unaware,
That the lowest boughs and the brushwood sheaf   5
Round the elm-tree bole are in tiny leaf,
While the chaffinch sings on the orchard bough
In England — now!

And after April, when May follows,
And the whitethroat builds, and all the swallows!   10
Hark, where my blossomed pear-tree in the hedge
Leans to the field and scatters on the clover
Blossoms and dewdrops — at the bent spray's edge —
That's the wise thrush; he sings each song twice over,
Lest you should think he never could recapture   15
The first fine careless rapture!
And though the fields look rough with hoary dew,
All will be gay when noontide wakes anew
The buttercups, the little children's dower
— Far brighter than this gaudy melon-flower!   20

HOME–THOUGHTS, FROM THE SEA

Nobly, nobly Cape Saint Vincent to the North-west
    died away;
Sunset ran, one glorious blood-red, reeking into Cadiz
    Bay;
Bluish 'mid the burning water, full in face Trafalgar lay;
In the dimmest North-east distance dawned Gibraltar
    grand and gray;
" Here and here did England help me: how can I help
    England? " — say,   5
Whoso turns as I, this evening, turn to God to praise and
    pray,
While Jove's planet rises yonder, silent over Africa.

THE ITALIAN IN ENGLAND

That second time they hunted me
From hill to plain, from shore to sea,
And Austria, hounding far and wide
Her blood-hounds through the country-side,
Breathed hot and instant on my trace, —   5
I made six days a hiding-place
Of that dry green old aqueduct
Where I and Charles, when boys, have plucked
The fire-flies from the roof above,
Bright creeping through the moss they love: 10
— How long it seems since Charles was lost!
Six days the soldiers crossed and crossed
The country in my very sight;
And when that peril ceased at night,

The sky broke out in red dismay 15
With signal fires; well, there I lay
Close covered o'er in my recess,
Up to the neck in ferns and cress,
Thinking on Metternich our friend,
And Charles's miserable end, 20
And much beside, two days; the third,
Hunger o'ercame me when I heard
The peasants from the village go
To work among the maize; you know,
With us in Lombardy, they bring 25
Provisions packed on mules, a string
With little bells that cheer their task,
And casks, and boughs on every cask
To keep the sun's heat from the wine;
These I let pass in jingling line, 30
And, close on them, dear noisy crew,
The peasants from the village, too;
For at the very rear would troop
Their wives and sisters in a group
To help, I knew.   When these had passed, 35
I threw my glove to strike the last,
Taking the chance: she did not start,
Much less cry out, but stooped apart,
One instant rapidly glanced round,
And saw me beckon from the ground; 40
A wild bush grows and hides my crypt;
She picked my glove up while she stripped
A branch off, then rejoined the rest
With that; my glove lay in her breast.
Then I drew breath: they disappeared: 45
It was for Italy I feared.

An hour, and she returned alone
Exactly where my glove was thrown.
Meanwhile came many thoughts; on me
Rested the hopes of Italy;   50
I had devised a certain tale
Which, when 'twas told her, could not fail
Persuade a peasant of its truth;
I meant to call a freak of youth
This hiding, and give hopes of pay,   55
And no temptation to betray.
But when I saw that woman's face,
Its calm simplicity of grace,
Our Italy's own attitude
In which she walked thus far, and stood,   60
Planting each naked foot so firm,
To crush the snake and spare the worm —
At first sight of her eyes, I said,
" I am that man upon whose head
They fix the price, because I hate   65
The Austrians over us: the State
Will give you gold — oh, gold so much! —
If you betray me to their clutch,
And be your death, for aught I know,
If once they find you saved their foe.   70
Now, you must bring me food and drink,
And also paper, pen, and ink,
And carry safe what I shall write
To Padua, which you'll reach at night
Before the duomo shuts; go in,   75
And wait till Tenebræ begin;
Walk to the third confessional,
Between the pillar and the wall,

And kneeling whisper, *Whence comes peace?*
Say it a second time, then cease;   80
And if the voice inside returns,
From Christ and Freedom; what concerns
The cause of Peace? — for answer, slip
My letter where you placed your lip;
Then come back happy we have done   85
Our mother service — I, the son,
As you the daughter of our land!"

   Three mornings more, she took her stand
In the same place, with the same eyes:
I was no surer of sunrise   90
Than of her coming.   We conferred
Of her own prospects, and I heard
She had a lover — stout and tall,
She said — then let her eyelids fall,
"He could do much" — as if some doubt   95
Entered her heart, — then, passing out,
"She could not speak for others, who
Had other thoughts; herself she knew:"
And so she brought me drink and food.
After four days, the scouts pursued   100
Another path; at last arrived
The help my Paduan friends contrived
To furnish me: she brought the news.
For the first time I could not choose
But kiss her hand, and lay my own   105
Upon her head — " This faith was shown
To Italy, our mother; she
Uses my hand and blesses thee."
She followed down to the sea-shore;
I left and never saw her more.   110

How very long since I have thought
Concerning — much less wished for — aught
Beside the good of Italy,
For which I live and mean to die!
I never was in love; and since   115
Charles proved false, what shall now convince
My inmost heart I have a friend?
However, if I pleased to spend
Real wishes on myself — say, three —
I know at least what one should be.   120
I would grasp Metternich until
I felt his red wet throat distil
In blood through these two hands.   And next
— Nor much for that am I perplexed —
Charles, perjured traitor, for his part,   125
Should die slow of a broken heart
Under his new employers.   Last
— Ah, there, what should I wish?   For fast
Do I grow old and out of strength.
If I resolved to seek at length   130
My father's house again, how scared
They all would look, and unprepared!
My brothers live in Austria's pay
— Disowned me long ago, men say;
And all my early mates who used   135
To praise me so — perhaps induced
More than one early step of mine —
Are turning wise: while some opine
" Freedom grows license," some suspect
" Haste breeds delay," and recollect   140
They always said, such premature
Beginnings never could endure!

So, with a sullen " All's for best,"
The land seems settling to its rest.
I think then, I should wish to stand   145
This evening in that dear, lost land,
Over the sea the thousand miles,
And know if yet that woman smiles
With the calm smile; some little farm
She lives in there, no doubt: what harm   150
If I sat on the door-side bench,
And, while her spindle made a trench
Fantastically in the dust,
Inquired of all her fortunes — just
Her children's ages and their names,   155
And what may be the husband's aims
For each of them.   I'd talk this out,
And sit there, for an hour about,
Then kiss her hand once more, and lay
Mine on her head, and go my way.   160

      So much for idle wishing — how
It steals the time !   To business now.

UP AT A VILLA — DOWN IN THE CITY

(AS DISTINGUISHED BY AN ITALIAN PERSON OF QUALITY)

HAD I but plenty of money, money enough and to spare,
The house for me, no doubt, were a house in the city-
      square ;
Ah, such a life, such a life, as one leads at the window
      there !

Something to see, by Bacchus, something to hear, at
     least!
There, the whole day long, one's life is a perfect feast;   5
While up at a villa one lives, I maintain it, no more than
     a beast.

Well now, look at our villa! stuck like the horn of a bull
Just on a mountain-edge as bare as the creature's skull,
Save a mere shag of a bush with hardly a leaf to pull!
— I scratch my own, sometimes, to see if the hair's
     turned wool.   10

But the city, oh the city — the square with the houses!
     Why?
They are stone-faced, white as a curd, there's something
     to take the eye!
Houses in four straight lines, not a single front awry;
You watch who crosses and gossips, who saunters, who
     hurries by;
Green blinds, as a matter of course, to draw when the sun
     gets high;   15
And the shops with fanciful signs which are painted
     properly.

What of a villa? Though winter be over in March by
     rights,
'Tis May perhaps ere the snow shall have withered well
     off the heights:
You've the brown ploughed land before, where the oxen
     steam and wheeze,
And the hills over-smoked behind by the faint gray
     olive-trees.   20

Is it better in May, I ask you? You've summer all at once;
In a day he leaps complete with a few strong April suns.
'Mid the sharp short emerald wheat, scarce risen three
    fingers well,
The wild tulip, at end of its tube, blows out its great red
    bell
Like a thin clear bubble of blood, for the children to pick
    and sell.   25
Is it ever hot in the square?   There's a fountain to spout
    and splash!
In the shade it sings and springs; in the shine such foam-
    bows flash
On the horses with curling fish-tails, that prance and
    paddle and pash
Round the lady atop in her conch — fifty gazers do not
    abash,
Though all that she wears is some weeds round her waist
    in a sort of sash.   30

All the year long at the villa, nothing to see though you
    linger,
Except yon cypress that points like death's lean lifted fore-
    finger.
Some think fireflies pretty, when they mix i' the corn and
    mingle,
Or thrid the stinking hemp till the stalks of it seem a-tingle.
Late August or early September, the stunning cicala is
    shrill,   35
And the bees keep their tiresome whine round the resinous
    firs on the hill.
Enough of the seasons, — I spare you the months of the
    fever and chill.

Ere you open your eyes in the city, the blessed church-bells
    begin :
No sooner the bells leave off than the diligence rattles in :
You get the·pick of the news, and it costs you never a
    pin.   40
By-and-by there's the travelling doctor gives pills, lets
    blood, draws teeth ;
Or the Pulcinello-trumpet breaks up the market beneath.
At the post-office such a scene-picture — the new play,
    piping hot !
And a notice how, only this morning, three liberal thieves
    were shot.
Above it, behold the Archbishop's most fatherly of
    rebukes,   45
And beneath with his crown and his lion, some little new
    law of the Duke's !
Or a sonnet with flowery marge, to the Reverend Don So-
    and-so
Who is Dante, Boccaccio, Petrarca, Saint Jerome and
    Cicero,
" And moreover," (the sonnet goes rhyming,) " the skirts
    of Saint Paul has reached.
Having preached us those six Lent-lectures more unctu-
    ous than ever he preached."   50
Noon strikes, — here sweeps the procession ! our Lady
    borne smiling and smart
With a pink gauze gown all spangles, and seven swords
    stuck in her heart !
Bang-whang-whang goes the drum, *tootle-te-tootle* the
    fife ;
No keeping one's haunches still : it's the greatest pleasure
    in life.

But bless you, it's dear — it's dear! fowls, wine, at
 double the rate.   55
They have clapped a new tax upon salt, and what oil pays
 passing the gate
It's a horror to think of.   And so, the villa for me, not the
 city!
Beggars can scarcely be choosers: but still — ah, the pity,
 the pity!
Look, two and two go the priests, then the monks with
 cowls and sandals,
And the penitents dressed in white shirts, a-holding
 the yellow candles;   60
One, he carries a flag up straight, and another a cross with
 handles,
And the Duke's guard brings up the rear, for the better
 prevention of scandals:
Bang-whang-whang goes the drum, *tootle-te-tootle* the fife.
Oh, a day in the city-square, there is no such pleasure in
 in life!

THE PIED PIPER OF HAMELIN

A CHILD'S STORY

I

Hamelin Town's in Brunswick,
 By famous Hanover city;
The river Weser, deep and wide,
Washes its wall on the southern side;
A pleasanter spot you never spied;   5
 But, when begins my ditty,
Almost five hundred years ago,
To see the townsfolk suffer so
 From vermin, was a pity.

II

Rats!   10
They fought the dogs and killed the cats,
     And bit the babies in the cradles,
And ate the cheeses out of the vats,
     And licked the soup from the cooks' own ladles,
Split open the kegs of salted sprats,   15
Made nests inside men's Sunday hats,
And even spoiled the women's chats
               By drowning their speaking
               With shrieking and squeaking
In fifty different sharps and flats.   20

III

At last the people in a body
     To the Town Hall came flocking.
" 'Tis clear," cried they, " our Mayor's a noddy;
And as for our Corporation — shocking
To think we buy gowns lined with ermine   25
For dolts that can't or won't determine
What's best to rid us of our vermin!
You hope, because you're old and obese,
To find in the furry civic robe ease?
Rouse up, sirs!   Give your brains a racking   30
To find the remedy we're lacking,
Or, sure as fate, we'll send you packing!"
At this the Mayor and Corporation
Quaked with a mighty consternation.

IV

An hour they sat in council,   35
     At length the Mayor broke silence:

" For a guilder I'd my ermine gown sell,
   I wish I were a mile hence!
It's easy to bid one rack one's brain —
I'm sure my poor head aches again,   40
I've scratched it so, and all in vain.
Oh for a trap, a trap, a trap!"
Just as he said this, what should hap
At the chamber door but a gentle tap?
" Bless us," cried the Mayor, " what's that?"   45
(With the Corporation as he sat,
Looking little though wondrous fat;
Nor brighter was his eye, nor moister
Than a too-long-opened oyster,
Save when at noon his paunch grew mutinous   50
For a plate of turtle green and glutinous)
" Only a scraping of shoes on the mat?
Anything like the sound of a rat
Makes my heart go pit-a-pat!"

V

" Come in!" — the Mayor cried, looking bigger: 55
And in did come the strangest figure!
His queer long coat from heel to head
Was half of yellow and half of red,
And he himself was tall and thin,
With sharp blue eyes, each like a pin,   60
And light loose hair, yet swarthy skin,
No tuft on cheek nor beard on chin,
But lips where smiles went out and in;
There was no guessing his kith and kin:
And nobody could enough admire   65
The tall man and his quaint attire.

Quoth one: " It's as my great-grandsire,
Starting up at the Trump of Doom's tone,
Had walked this way from his painted tombstone!"

VI

He advanced to the council-table: 70
And, " Please your honours," said he, " I'm able,
By means of a secret charm, to draw
    All creatures living beneath the sun,
    That creep or swim or fly or run,
After me so as you never saw!   75
And I chiefly use my charm
On creatures that do people harm,
The mole and toad and newt and viper;
And people call me the Pied Piper."
(And here they noticed round his neck   80
    A scarf of red and yellow stripe,
To match with his coat of the self-same cheque;
    And at the scarf's end hung a pipe;
And his fingers, they noticed, were ever straying
As if impatient to be playing   85
Upon this pipe, as low it dangled
Over his vesture so old-fangled.)
" Yet," said he, " poor piper as I am,
In Tartary I freed the Cham,
    Last June, from his huge swarms of gnats;   90
I eased in Asia the Nizam
    Of a monstrous brood of vampire-bats:
And as for what your brain bewilders,
    If I can rid your town of rats
Will you give me a thousand guilders?"   95

" One? fifty thousand!" — was the exclamation
Of the astonished Mayor and Corporation.

VII

Into the street the Piper stept,
 Smiling first a little smile,
As if he knew what magic slept   100
 In his quiet pipe the while;
Then, like a musical adept,
To blow the pipe his lips he wrinkled,
And green and blue his sharp eyes twinkled,
Like a candle-flame where salt is sprinkled;   105
And ere three shrill notes the pipe uttered,
You heard as if an army muttered;
And the muttering grew to a grumbling;
And the grumbling grew to a mighty rumbling;
And out of the houses the rats came tumbling.   110
Great rats, small rats, lean rats, brawny rats,
Brown rats, black rats, gray rats, tawny rats,
Grave old plodders, gay young friskers,
 Fathers, mothers, uncles, cousins,
Cocking tails and pricking whiskers,   115
 Families by tens and dozens,
Brothers, sisters, husbands, wives —
Followed the Piper for their lives.
From street to street he piped advancing,
And step for step they followed dancing,   120
Until they came to the river Weser,
 Wherein all plunged and perished!
— Save one who, stout as Julius Cæsar,
Swam across and lived to carry
 (As he, the manuscript he cherished)   125

To Rat-land home his commentary :
Which was, " At the first shrill notes of the pipe,
I heard a sound as of scraping tripe,
And putting apples, wondrous ripe,
Into a cider-press's gripe :　　　　　　　　130
And a moving away of pickle-tub-boards,
And a leaving ajar of conserve-cupboards,
And a drawing the corks of train-oil-flasks,
And a breaking the hoops of butter-casks :
And it seemed as if a voice　　　　　　　135
　(Sweeter far than by harp or by psaltery
Is breathed) called out, ' Oh rats, rejoice !
　The world is grown to one vast dry saltery !
So munch on, crunch on, take your nuncheon,
Breakfast, supper, dinner, luncheon !'　　　140
And just as a bulky sugar-puncheon,
All ready staved, like a great sun shone
Glorious scarce an inch before me,
Just as methought it said, ' Come, bore me !'
— I found the Weser rolling o'er me."　　　145

VIII

You should have heard the Hamelin people
Ringing the bells till they rocked the steeple.
" Go," cried the Mayor, " and get long poles,
Poke out the nests and block up the holes !
Consult with carpenters and builders,　　　150
And leave in our town not even a trace
Of the rats !" — when suddenly, up the face
Of the Piper perked in the market-place,
With a, " First, if you please, my thousand guilders !"

IX

A thousand guilders! The Mayor looked blue;   155
So did the Corporation too.
For council dinners made rare havoc
With Claret, Moselle, Vin-de-Grave, Hock;
And half the money would replenish
Their cellar's biggest butt with Rhenish.   160
To pay this sum to a wandering fellow
With a gipsy coat of red and yellow!
" Beside," quoth the Mayor with a knowing wink,
" Our business was done at the river's brink;
We saw with our eyes the vermin sink,   165
And what's dead can't come to life, I think.
So, friend, we're not the folks to shrink
From the duty of giving you something for drink,
And a matter of money to put in your poke;
But as for the guilders, what we spoke   170
Of them, as you very well know, was in joke.
Beside, our losses have made us thrifty.
A thousand guilders! Come, take fifty!"

X

The Piper's face fell, and he cried,
" No trifling! I can't wait, beside!   175
I've promised to visit by dinner time
Bagdat, and accept the prime
Of the Head-Cook's pottage, all he's rich in,
For having left, in the Caliph's kitchen,
Of a nest of scorpions no survivor: 180
With him I proved no bargain-driver,
With you, don't think I'll bate a stiver!

And folks who put me in a passion
May find me pipe after another fashion."

XI

" How? " cried the Mayor, " d'ye think I brook   185
Being worse treated than a Cook?
Insulted by a lazy ribald
With idle pipe and vesture piebald?
You threaten us, fellow?   Do your worst,
Blow your pipe there till you burst!"   190

XII

Once more he stept into the street,
    And to his lips again
Laid his long pipe of smooth straight cane;
    And ere he blew three notes (such sweet
Soft notes as yet musician's cunning   195
    Never gave the enraptured air)
There was a rustling that seemed like a bustling
Of merry crowds justling at pitching and hustling;
Small feet were pattering, wooden shoes clattering,
Little hands clapping and little tongues chattering,   200
And, like fowls in a farm-yard when barley is scattering,
Out came the children running.
All the little boys and girls,
With rosy cheeks and flaxen curls,
And sparkling eyes and teeth like pearls,   205
Tripping and skipping, ran merrily after
The wonderful music with shouting and laughter.

XIII

The Mayor was dumb and the Council stood
As if they were changed into blocks of wood,

Unable to move a step, or cry   210
To the children merrily skipping by,
— Could only follow with the eye
That joyous crowd at the Piper's back.
But how the Mayor was on the rack,
And the wretched Council's bosoms beat,   215
As the Piper turned from the High Street
To where the Weser rolled its waters
Right in the way of their sons and daughters!
However he turned from South to West,
And to Koppelberg Hill his steps addressed,   220
And after him the children pressed;
Great was the joy in every breast.
"He never can cross that mighty top!
He's forced to let the piping drop,
And we shall see our children stop!"   225
When, lo, as they reached the mountain-side,
A wondrous portal opened wide,
As if a cavern was suddenly hollowed;
And the Piper advanced and the children followed,
And when all were in to the very last,   230
The door in the mountain-side shut fast.
Did I say, all? No! One was lame,
   And could not dance the whole of the way;
And in after years, if you would blame
   His sadness, he was used to say, —   235
"It's dull in our town since my playmates left!
I can't forget that I'm bereft
Of all the pleasant sights they see,
Which the Piper also promised me.
For he led us, he said, to a joyous land,   240
Joining the town and just at hand,

Where waters gushed and fruit-trees grew
And flowers put forth a fairer hue,
And everything was strange and new;
The sparrows were brighter than peacocks here,   245
And their dogs outran our fallow deer,
And honey-bees had lost their stings,
And horses were born with eagles' wings:
And just as I became assured
My lame foot would be speedily cured,   250
The music stopped and I stood still,
And found myself outside the hill,
Left alone against my will,
To go now limping as before,
And never hear of that country more!"   255

XIV

Alas, alas for Hamelin!
    There came into many a burgher's pate
    A text which says that heaven's gate
    Opes to the rich at as easy rate
As the needle's eye takes a camel in!   260
The Mayor sent East, West, North, and South,
To offer the Piper, by word of mouth,
    Wherever it was men's lot to find him,
Silver and gold to his heart's content,
If he'd only return the way he went,   265
    And bring the children behind him.
But when they saw 'twas a lost endeavour,
And Piper and dancers were gone forever,
They made a decree that lawyers never
    Should think their records dated duly   270
If, after the day of the month and year,

These words did not as well appear,
"And so long after what happened here
  On the Twenty-second of July,
Thirteen hundred and seventy-six:"   275
And the better in memory to fix
The place of the children's last retreat,
They called it, the Pied Piper's Street —
Where any one playing on pipe or tabor
Was sure for the future to lose his labour.   280
Nor suffered they hostelry or tavern
  To shock with mirth a street so solemn;
But opposite the place of the cavern
  They wrote the story on a column,
And on the great church-window painted   285
The same, to make the world acquainted
How their children were stolen away,
And there it stands to this very day.
And I must not omit to say
That in Transylvania there's a tribe   290
Of alien people who ascribe
The outlandish ways and dress
On which their neighbours lay such stress,
To their fathers and mothers having risen
Out of some subterraneous prison   295
Into which they were trepanned
Long time ago in a mighty band
Out of Hamelin town in Brunswick land,
But how or why, they don't understand.

XV

So, Willy, let me and you be wipers   300
Of scores out with all men — especially pipers!

And, whether they pipe us free frόm rats or frόm mice,
If we've promised them aught, let us keep our promise!

"DE GUSTIBUS ——"

Your ghost will walk, you lover of trees,
    (If our loves remain)
    In an English lane,
By a cornfield-side a-flutter with poppies.
Hark, those two in the hazel coppice —   5
A boy and a girl, if the good fates please,
    Making love, say, —
    The happier they!
Draw yourself up from the light of the moon,
And let them pass, as they will too soon,   10
    With the bean-flowers' boon,
    And the blackbird's tune,
    And May, and June!

What I love best in all the world
Is a castle, precipice-encurled,   15
In a gash of the wind-grieved Apennine.
Or look for me, old fellow of mine,
(If I get my head from out the mouth
O' the grave, and loose my spirit's bands,
And come again to the land of lands) —   20
In a sea-side house to the farther South,
Where the baked cicala dies of drouth,
And one sharp tree — 'tis a cypress — stands,
By the many hundred years red-rusted,
Rough iron-spiked, ripe fruit-o'ercrusted,   25

My sentinel to guard the sands
To the water's edge.   For, what expands
Before the house, but the great opaque
Blue breadth of sea without a break?
While, in the house, for ever crumbles   30
Some fragment of the frescoed walls,
From blisters where a scorpion sprawls.
A girl bare-footed brings, and tumbles
Down on the pavement, green-flesh melons,
And says there's news to-day — the king   35
Was shot at, touched in the liver-wing,
Goes with his Bourbon arm in a sling:
— She hopes they have not caught the felons.
Italy, my Italy!
Queen Mary's saying serves for me —   40
      (When fortune's malice
      Lost her — Calais) —
Open my heart and you will see
Graved inside of it, "Italy."
Such lovers old are I and she: 45
So it always was, so shall ever be!

MEMORABILIA

Ah, did you once see Shelley plain,
    And did he stop and speak to you,
And did you speak to him again?
    How strange it seems and new!

But you were living before that,   5
    And also you are living after;
And the memory I started at —
    My starting moves your laughter.

I crossed a moor, with a name of its own
   And a certain use in the world no doubt,   10
Yet a hand's-breadth of it shines alone
   'Mid the blank miles round about:

For there I picked up on the heather,
   And there I put inside my breast
A moulted feather, an eagle-feather!   15
   Well, I forget the rest.

INSTANS TYRANNUS

I

OF the million or two, more or less,
I rule and possess,
One man, for some cause undefined,
Was least to my mind.

II

I struck him, he grovelled of course —   5
For, what was his force?
I pinned him to earth with my weight
And persistence of hate:
And he lay, would not moan, would not curse,
As his lot might be worse.   10

III

"Were the object less mean, would he stand
At the swing of my hand!
For obscurity helps him and blots
The hole where he squats."
So, I set my five wits on the stretch   15
To inveigle the wretch.

All in vain!   Gold and jewels I threw,
Still he couched there perdue;
I tempted his blood and his flesh,
Hid in roses my mesh,   20
Choicest cates and the flagon's best spilth:
Still he kept to his filth.

IV

Had he kith now or kin, were access
To his heart, did I press:
Just a son or a mother to seize!   25
No such booty as these.
Were it simply a friend to pursue
'Mid my million or two,
Who could pay me in person or pelf
What he owes me himself!   30
No: I could not but smile through my chafe:
For the fellow lay safe
As his mates do, the midge and the nit,
— Through minuteness, to wit.

V

Then a humor more great took its place   35
At the thought of his face,
The droops, the low cares of the mouth,
The trouble uncouth
'Twixt the brows, all that air one is fain
To put out of its pain.   40
And, "no!" I admonished myself,
"Is one mocked by an elf,
Is one baffled by toad or by rat?
The gravamen's in that!

How the lion, who crouches to suit   45
His back to my foot,
Would admire that I stand in debate!
But the small turns the great
If it vexes you, — that is the thing!
Toad or rat vex the king?   50
Though I waste half my realm to unearth
Toad or rat, 'tis well worth!"

VI

So, I soberly laid my last plan
To extinguish the man.
Round his creep-hole, with never a break,   55
Ran my fires for his sake;
Over-head, did my thunder combine
With my underground mine:
Till I looked from my labor content
To enjoy the event.   60

VII

When sudden . . . how think ye, the end?
Did I say " without friend "?
Say rather, from marge to blue marge
The whole sky grew his targe
With the sun's self for visible boss,   65
While an Arm ran across
Which the earth heaved beneath like a breast
Where the wretch was safe prest!
Do you see?   Just my vengeance complete,
The man sprang to his feet,   70
Stood erect, caught at God's skirts, and prayed!
— So, *I* was afraid!

TRAY

Sing me a hero! Quench my thirst
Of souls, ye bards!
                    Quoth Bard the first:
" Sir Olaf, the good knight, did don
His helm and eke his habergeon " . . .
Sir Olaf and his bard —!   5

" That sin-scathed brow " (quoth Bard the second),
" That eye wide ope as though Fate beckoned
My hero to some steep, beneath
Which precipice smiled tempting death " . . .
You too without your host have reckoned!   10

" A beggar-child " (let's hear this third!)
" Sat on a quay's edge: like a bird
Sang to herself at careless play,
And fell into the stream. ' Dismay!
Help, you the standers-by! ' None stirred.   15

" Bystanders reason, think of wives
And children ere they risk their lives.
Over the balustrade has bounced
A mere instinctive dog, and pounced
Plumb on the prize. ' How well he dives!   20

" ' Up he comes with the child, see, tight
In mouth, alive too, clutched from quite
A depth of ten feet — twelve, I bet!
Good dog! What, off again? There's yet
Another child to save? All right!   25

" ' How strange we saw no other fall!
It's instinct in the animal.
Good dog! But he's a long while under:
If he got drowned I should not wonder —
Strong current, that against the wall!   30

" ' Here he comes, holds in mouth this time
— What may the thing be? Well, that's prime!
Now, did you ever? Reason reigns
In man alone, since all Tray's pains
Have fished — the child's doll from the slime! '   35

" And so, amid the laughter gay,
Trotted my hero off, — old Tray, —
Till somebody, prerogatived
With reason, reasoned: ' Why he dived,
His brain would show us, I should say.   40

" ' John, go and catch — or, if needs be,
Purchase — that animal for me!
By vivisection, at expense
Of half-an-hour and eighteenpence,
How brain secretes dog's soul, we'll see! ' "   45

CAVALIER TUNES

I

MARCHING ALONG

KENTISH Sir Byng stood for his King,
Bidding the crop-headed Parliament swing:
And, pressing a troop unable to stoop
And see the rogues flourish and honest folk droop,

Marched them along, fifty-score strong,   5
Great-hearted gentlemen, singing this song.

God for King Charles! Pym and such carles
To the Devil that prompts 'em their treasonous parles!
Cavaliers, up! Lips from the cup,
Hands from the pasty, nor bite take nor sup   10
Till you're —
     CHORUS. — *Marching along, fifty-score strong,*
                Great-hearted gentlemen, singing this song.

Hampden to hell, and his obsequies' knell
Serve Hazelrig, Fiennes, and young Harry as well!
England, good cheer! Rupert is near!   15
Kentish and loyalists, keep we not here,
     CHORUS. — *Marching along, fifty-score strong,*
                Great-hearted gentlemen, singing this song?

Then, God for King Charles! Pym and his snarls
To the Devil that pricks on such pestilent carles!   20
Hold by the right, you double your might;
So, onward to Nottingham, fresh for the fight,
     CHORUS. — *March we along, fifty-score strong,*
                Great-hearted gentlemen, singing this song!

II

GIVE A ROUSE

King Charles, and who'll do him right now?
King Charles, and who's ripe for fight now?
Give a rouse: here's, in hell's despite now,
    King Charles!

Who gave me the goods that went since?   5
Who raised me the house that sank once?
Who helped me to gold I spent since?
Who found me in wine you drank once?
> CHORUS. —
>> *King Charles, and who'll do him right now?*
>> *King Charles, and who's ripe for fight now?*   10
>> *Give a rouse: here's, in hell's despite now,*
>> *King Charles!*

To whom used my boy George quaff else,
By the old fool's side that begot him?
For whom did he cheer and laugh else,   15
While Noll's damned troopers shot him?
> CHORUS. —
>> *King Charles, and who'll do him right now?*
>> *King Charles, and who's ripe for fight now?*
>> *Give a rouse: here's, in hell's despite now,*
>> *King Charles!*   20

III

BOOT AND SADDLE

Boot, saddle, to horse, and away!
Rescue my castle before the hot day
Brightens to blue from its silvery gray.
> CHORUS. — *Boot, saddle, to horse, and away!*

Ride past the suburbs, asleep as you'd say;   5
Many's the friend there, will listen and pray
" God's luck to gallants that strike up the lay —
> CHORUS. — *Boots, saddle, to horse, and away!* "

Forty miles off, like a roebuck at bay,
Flouts Castle Brancepeth the Roundheads' array :   10
Who laughs, " Good fellows ere this, by my fay,
    CHORUS. — *Boot, saddle, to horse, and away !* "

Who? My wife Gertrude ; that, honest and gay,
Laughs when you talk of surrendering, " Nay !
I've better counsellors ; what counsel they?   15
    CHORUS. — *Boot, saddle, to horse, and away !* "

HERVÉ RIEL

I

ON the sea and at the Hogue, sixteen hundred ninety-two,
  Did the English fight the French, — woe to France !
And, the thirty-first of May, helter-skelter through the
    blue,
Like a crowd of frightened porpoises a shoal of sharks
    pursue,
  Came crowding ship on ship to Saint-Malo on the
    Rance,   5
With the English fleet in view.

II

'Twas the squadron that escaped, with the victor in full
    chase ;
  First and foremost of the drove, in his great ship, Dam-
    freville ;
      Close on him fled, great and small,
      Twenty-two good ships in all ;   10
And they signalled to the place
" Help the winners of a race !

Get us guidance, give us harbour, take us quick — or,
     quicker still,
Here's the English can and will ! ' "

III

Then the pilots of the place put out brisk and leapt on
     board ;   15
  " Why, what hope or chance have ships like these to
     pass ? " laughed they :
" Rocks to starboard, rocks to port, all the passage scarred
     and scored, —
Shall the ' Formidable ' here, with her twelve and eighty
     guns,
  Think to make the river-mouth by the single narrow way,
Trust to enter — where 'tis ticklish for a craft of twenty
     tons,   20
     And with flow at full beside ?
     Now, 'tis slackest ebb of tide.
  Reach the mooring ?   Rather say,
While rock stands or water runs,
  Not a ship will leave the bay ! "   25

IV

Then was called a council straight.
Brief and bitter the debate :
" Here's the English at our heels ; would you have them
     take in tow
All that's left us of the fleet, linked together stern and bow,
For a prize to Plymouth Sound ?   30
Better run the ships aground ! "
     (Ended Damfreville his speech.)

" Not a minute more to wait !
   Let the Captains all and each
   Shove ashore, then blow up, burn the vessels on the
     beach !   35
France must undergo her fate.

V

Give the word ! "   But no such word
Was ever spoke or heard ;
   For up stood, for out stepped, for in struck amid all
     these
— A Captain? A Lieutenant? A Mate — first, second,
     third?   40
   No such man of mark, and meet
   With his betters to compete !
   But a simple Breton sailor pressed by Tourville for the
     fleet,
A poor coasting-pilot he, Hervé Riel the Croisickese.

VI

And " What mockery or malice have we here? " cries
     Hervé Riel :   45
   " Are you mad, you Malouins? Are you cowards,
     fools, or rogues?
Talk to me of rocks and shoals, me who took the soundings,
     tell
On my fingers every bank, every shallow, every swell
   'Twixt the offing here and Grève where the river dis-
     embogues?
Are you bought by English gold? Is it love the lying's
     for?   50

Morn and eve, night and day,
Have I piloted your bay,
Entered free and anchored fast at the foot of Solidor.
  Burn the fleet and ruin France?   That were worse than
    fifty Hogues!
    Sirs, they know I speak the truth! Sirs, believe
    me there's a way!   55
Only let me lead the line,
  Have the biggest ship to steer,
  Get this ' Formidable ' clear,
Make the others follow mine,
And I lead them, most and least, by a passage I know
  well,   60
  Right to Solidor past Grève,
    And there lay them safe and sound;
And if one ship misbehave, —
— Keel so much as grate the ground,
Why, I've nothing but my life, — here's my head!"
cries Hervé Riel.   65

VII

Not a minute more to wait.
" Steer us in, then, small and great!
  Take the helm, lead the line, save the squadron!" cried
  its chief.
Captains, give the sailor place!
  He is Admiral, in brief.   70
Still the north-wind, by God's grace!
See the noble fellow's face
As the big ship, with a bound,
Clears the entry like a hound,

Keeps the passage, as its inch of way were the wide sea's
    profound!   75
  See, safe thro' shoal and rock,
  How they follow in a flock,
Not a ship that misbehaves, not a keel that grates the
    ground,
  Not a spar that comes to grief!
The peril, see, is past,   80
All are harboured to the last,
And just as Hervé Riel hollas " Anchor! " — sure as fate,
Up the English come, — too late!

VIII

So, the storm subsides to calm:
  They see the green trees wave   85
  On the heights o'erlooking Grève.
Hearts that bled are stanched with balm.
" Just our rapture to enhance,
  Let the English rake the bay,
Gnash their teeth and glare askance   90
  As they cannonade away!
'Neath rampired Solidor pleasant riding on the Rance! "
How hope succeeds despair on each Captain's countenance!
Out burst all with one accord,
  " This is Paradise for Hell!   95
  Let France, let France's King
  Thank the man that did the thing! "
What a shout, and all one word, " Hervé Riel! "
As he stepped in front once more,
  Not a symptom of surprise   100
  In the frank blue Breton eyes,
Just the same man as before.

IX

Then said Damfreville, " My friend,
I must speak out at the end,
  Though I find the speaking hard.   105
Praise is deeper than the lips:
You have saved the King his ships,
  You must name your own reward.
'Faith, our sun was near eclipse!
Demand whate'er you will,   110
France remains your debtor still.
Ask to heart's content and have ! or my name's not Dam-
    freville."

X

Then a beam of fun outbroke
On the bearded mouth that spoke,
As the honest heart laughed through   115
Those frank eyes of Breton blue:
" Since I needs must say my say,
  Since on board the duty's done,
    And from Malo Roads to Croisic Point, what is it but
    a run ? —
Since 'tis ask and have, I may —   120
  Since the others go ashore —
Come !   A good whole holiday !
  Leave to go and see my wife, whom I call the Belle
    Aurore ! "
  That he asked and that he got, — nothing more.

XI

Name and deed alike are lost: 125
Not a pillar nor a post

In his Croisic keeps alive the feat as it befell;
Not a head in white and black
On a single fishing-smack,
In memory of the man but for whom had gone to wrack 130
    All that France saved from the fight whence England
    bore the bell.
Go to Paris: rank on rank
    Search the heroes flung pell-mell
On the Louvre, face and flank!
    You shall look long enough ere you come to Hervé
    Riel.   135
So, for better and for worse,
Hervé Riel, accept my verse!
In my verse, Hervé Riel, do thou once more
Save the squadron, honour France, love thy wife the Belle
    Aurore!

PHEIDIPPIDES

Χαίρετε, νικῶμεν

First I salute this soil of the blessed, river and rock!
Gods of my birthplace, dæmons and heroes, honour to all!
Then I name thee, claim thee for our patron, co-equal
    in praise
— Ay, with Zeus the Defender, with Her of the ægis and
    spear!
Also, ye of the bow and the buskin, praised be your peer, 5
Now, henceforth and forever, — O latest to whom I up-
    raise
Hand and heart and voice! For Athens, leave pasture
    and flock!
Present to help, potent to save, Pan — patron I call!

Archons of Athens, topped by the tettix, see, I return!

See, 'tis myself here standing alive, no spectre that
    speaks!   10

Crowned with the myrtle, did you command me, Athens
    and you,

" Run, Pheidippides, run and race, reach Sparta for aid!

Persia has come, we are here, where is She? "   Your com-
    mand I obeyed,

Ran and raced: like stubble, some field which a fire runs
    through,

Was the space between city and city: two days, two
    nights did I burn   15

Over the hills, under the dales, down pits and up peaks.

Into their midst I broke: breath served but for " Persia
    has come!

Persia bids Athens proffer slaves'-tribute, water and
    earth;

Razed to the ground is Eretria — but Athens, shall Athens
    sink,

Drop into dust and die — the flower of Hellas utterly die,   20

Die, with the wide world spitting at Sparta, the stupid,
    the stander-by?

Answer me quick, what help, what hand do you stretch
    o'er destruction's brink?

How, — when?   No care for my limbs! — there's light-
    ning in all and some —

Fresh and fit your message to bear, once lips give it birth! "

O my Athens — Sparta love thee?   Did Sparta respond?   25

Every face of her leered in a furrow of envy, mistrust,

Malice, — each eye of her gave me its glitter of gratified
    hate!

Gravely they turned to take counsel, to cast for excuses. I stood

Quivering, — the limbs of me fretting as fire frets, an inch from dry wood:

"Persia has come, Athens asks aid, and still they debate? 30

Thunder, thou Zeus! Athené, are Spartans a quarry beyond

Swing of thy spear? Phoibos and Artemis, clang them 'Ye must'!"

No bolt launched from Olympos! Lo, their answer at last!

" Has Persia come, — does Athens ask aid, — may Sparta befriend?

Nowise precipitate judgment — too weighty the issue at stake! 35

Count we no time lost time which lags through respect to the gods!

Ponder that precept of old, ' No warfare, whatever the odds

In your favour, so long as the moon, half-orbed, is unable to take

Full-circle her state in the sky!' Already she rounds to it fast:

Athens must wait, patient as we — who judgment suspend." 40

Athens, — except for that sparkle, — thy name, I had mouldered to ash!

That sent a blaze through my blood; off, off and away was I back,

— Not one word to waste, one look to lose on the false and
the vile!

Yet "O gods of my land!" I cried, as each hillock and
plain,

Wood and stream, I knew, I named, rushing past them
again,   45

" Have ye kept faith, proved mindful of honours we paid
you erewhile?

Vain was the filleted victim, the fulsome libation! Too
rash

Love in its choice, paid you so largely service so slack!

" Oak and olive and bay, — I bid you cease to enwreathe

Brows made bold by your leaf! Fade at the Persian's
foot,   50

You that, our patrons were pledged, should never adorn a
slave!

Rather I hail thee, Parnes, — trust to thy wild waste tract!

Treeless, herbless, lifeless mountain! What matter if
slacked

My speed may hardly be, for homage to crag and to cave

No diety deigns to drape with verdure? at least I can
breathe,   55

Fear in thee no fraud from the blind, no lie from the
mute!"

Such my cry as, rapid, I ran over Parnes' ridge;

Gully and gap I clambered and cleared till, sudden, a bar

Jutted, a stoppage of stone against me, blocking the way.

Right! for I minded the hollow to traverse, the fissure
across :   60

" Where I could enter, there I depart by! Night in the
fosse?

Athens to aid? Though the dive were through Erebos,
   thus I obey —
Out of the day dive, into the day as bravely arise! No
   bridge
Better!"—when—ha! what was it I came on, of
   wonders that are?

There, in the cool of a cleft, sat he — majestical Pan: 65
Ivy drooped wanton, kissed his head, moss cushioned his
   hoof:
All the great god was good in the eyes grave-kindly — the
   curl
Carved on the bearded cheek, amused at a mortal's awe,
As, under the human trunk, the goat-thighs grand I
   saw.
"Halt, Pheidippides!"—halt I did, my brain of a
   whirl: 70
"Hither to me! Why pale in my presence?" he gracious
   began:
"How is it,—Athens, only in Hellas, holds me aloof?

"Athens, she only, rears me no fane, makes me no feast!
Wherefore? Than I what godship to Athens more help-
   ful of old?
Ay, and still, and for ever her friend! Test Pan, trust
   me!   75
Go, bid Athens take heart, laugh Persia to scorn, have
   faith
In the temples and tombs! Go, say to Athens, 'The
   Goat-God saith:
When Persia — so much as strews not the soil — is cast in
   the sea,

Then praise Pan who fought in the ranks with your most
    and least,
Goat-thigh to greaved-thigh, made one cause with the
    free and the bold!'   80

"Say Pan saith: ' Let this, foreshowing the place, be the
    pledge!'"
(Gay, the liberal hand held out this herbage I bear
— Fennel — I grasped it a-tremble with dew — whatever
    it bode)
"While, as for thee" . . . But enough! He was gone.
    If I ran hitherto —
Be sure that, the rest of my journey, I ran no longer, but
    flew.   85
Parnes to Athens — earth no more, the air was my road:
Here am I back. Praise Pan, we stand no more on the
    razor's edge!
Pan for Athens, Pan for me!   I too have a guerdon rare!

———————

Then spoke Miltiades,   "And thee, best runner of Greece,
Whose limbs did duty indeed, — what gift is promised
    thyself?   90
Tell it us straightway, — Athens the mother demands of
    her son!"
Rosily blushed the youth: he paused: but, lifting at length
His eyes from the ground, it seemed as he gathered the
    rest of his strength
Into the utterance — " Pan spoke thus: ' For what thou
    hast done
Count on a worthy reward! Henceforth be allowed thee
    release   95

From the racer's toil, no vulgar reward in praise or in
pelf ! '

" I am bold to believe, Pan means reward the most to my
mind !
Fight I shall, with our foremost, wherever this fennel
may grow, —
Pound — Pan helping us — Persia to dust, and, under the
deep,
Whelm her away for ever; and then, — no Athens to
save, — 100
Marry a certain maid, I know keeps faith to the brave, —
Hie to my house and home : and, when my children shall
creep
Close to my knees, — recount how the God was awful yet
kind,
Promised their sire reward to the full — rewarding him —
so ! "

Unforeseeing one ! Yes, he fought on the Marathon
day : 105
So, when Persia was dust, all cried " To Akropolis !
Run, Pheidippides, one race more ! the meed is thy due !
' Athens is saved, thank Pan,' go shout ! " He flung down
his shield,
Ran like fire once more : and the space 'twixt the Fennel-
field
And Athens was stubble again, a field which a fire runs
through, 110
Till in he broke : " Rejoice, we conquer ! " Like wine
through clay,
Joy in his blood bursting his heart, he died — the bliss !

So, to this day, when friend meets friend, the word of
　salute
Is still "Rejoice!"—his word which brought rejoicing
　indeed.
So is Pheidippides happy for ever,—the noble strong
　man　　　　　　　　　　　　　　　　　　　115
Who could race like a god, bear the face of a god, whom
　a god loved so well;
He saw the land saved he had helped to save, and was
　suffered to tell
Such tidings, yet never decline, but, gloriously as he began,
So to end gloriously—once to shout, thereafter be mute:
"Athens is saved!"—Pheidippides dies in the shout
　for his meed.　　　　　　　　　　　　　　120

THE PATRIOT

IT was roses, roses, all the way,
　With myrtle mixed in my path like mad:
The house-roofs seemed to heave and sway,
　The church-spires flamed, such flags they had,
A year ago on this very day.　　　　　　　　5

The air broke into a mist with bells,
　The old walls rocked with the crowd and cries.
Had I said, "Good folk, mere noise repels—
　But give me your sun from yonder skies!"
They had answered, "And afterward, what else?"　10

Alack, it was I who leaped at the sun
　To give it my loving friends to keep!
Naught man could do, have I left undone:
　And you see my harvest, what I reap
This very day, now a year is run.　　　　　　15

There's nobody on the house-tops now —
    Just a palsied few at the windows set;
For the best of the sight is, all allow,
    At the Shambles' Gate — or, better yet,
By the very scaffold's foot, I trow.   20

I go in the rain, and, more than needs,
    A rope cuts both my wrists behind;
And I think, by the feel, my forehead bleeds,
    For they fling, whoever has a mind,
Stones at me for my year's misdeeds.   25

Thus I entered, and thus I go!
    In triumphs, people have dropped down dead.
" Paid by the world, what dost thou owe
    Me? " — God might question; now instead,
'Tis God shall repay: I am safer so.   30

RABBI BEN EZRA

GROW old along with me!
    The best is yet to be,
The last of life, for which the first was made:
    Our times are in His hand
    Who saith " A whole I planned,   5
Youth shows but half; trust God: see all nor be afraid! "

    Not that, amassing flowers,
    Youth sighed " Which rose make ours,
Which lily leave and then as best recall? "
    Not that, admiring stars,   10
    It yearned " Nor Jove, nor Mars;
Mine be some figured flame which blends, transcends
    them all! "

Not for such hopes and fears
Annulling youth's brief years,
Do I remonstrate : folly wide the mark !   15
Rather I prize the doubt
Low kinds exist without,
Finished and finite clods, untroubled by a spark.

Poor vaunt of life indeed,
Were man but formed to feed   20
On joy, to solely seek and find and feast :
Such feasting ended, then
As sure an end to men ;
Irks care the crop-full bird? Frets doubt the maw-
    crammed beast ?

Rejoice we are allied   25
To That which doth provide
And not partake, effect and not receive !
A spark disturbs our clod ;
Nearer we hold of God
Who gives, than of His tribes that take, I must believe.   30

Then, welcome each rebuff
That turns earth's smoothness rough,
Each sting that bids nor sit nor stand but go !
Be our joys three-parts pain !
Strive, and hold cheap the strain ;   35
Learn, nor account the pang ; dare, never grudge the throe !

For thence, — a paradox
Which comforts while it mocks, —
Shall life succeed in that it seems to fail :
What I aspired to be,   40
And was not, comforts me :
A brute I might have been, but would not sink i' the scale.

What is he but a brute
Whose flesh has soul to suit,
Whose spirit works lest arms and legs want play?   45
To man, propose this test —
Thy body at its best,
How far can that project thy soul on its lone way?

Yet gifts should prove their use:
I own the Past profuse   50
Of power each side, perfection every turn:
Eyes, ears took in their dole,
Brain treasured up the whole;
Should not the heart beat once "How good to live and
learn"?

Not once beat "Praise be Thine!   55
I see the whole design,
I, who saw power, see now Love perfect too:
Perfect I call Thy plan:
Thanks that I was a man!
Maker, remake, complete, — I trust what Thou shalt
do!"   60

For pleasant is this flesh;
Our soul, in its rose-mesh
Pulled ever to the earth, still yearns for rest:
Would we some prize might hold
To match those manifold   65
Possessions of the brute, — gain most, as we did best!

Let us not always say
"Spite of this flesh to-day
I strove, made head, gained ground upon the whole!"

As the bird wings and sings,   70
Let us cry " All good things
Are ours, nor soul helps flesh more, now, than flesh helps
        soul ! "

Therefore I summon age
To grant youth's heritage,
Life's struggle having so far reached its term :   75
Thence shall I pass, approved
A man, for aye removed
From the developed brute ; a god though in the germ.

And I shall thereupon
Take rest, ere I be gone   80
Once more on my adventure brave and new :
Fearless and unperplexed,
When I wage battle next,
What weapons to select, what armour to indue.

Youth ended, I shall try   85
My gain or loss thereby ;
Leave the fire ashes, what survives is gold :
And I shall weigh the same,
Give life its praise or blame :
Young, all lay in dispute ; I shall know, being old.   90

For note, when evening shuts,
A certain moment cuts
The deed off, calls the glory from the gray :
A whisper from the west
Shoots — " Add this to the rest,   95
Take it and try its worth : here dies another day."

So, still within this life,
Though lifted o'er its strife,
Let me discern, compare, pronounce at last,
" This rage was right i' the main, 100
That acquiescence vain:
The Future I may face now I have proved the Past."

For more is not reserved
To man, with soul just nerved
To act to-morrow what he learns to-day: 105
Here, work enough to watch
The Master work, and catch
Hints of the proper craft, tricks of the tool's true play.

As it was better, youth
Should strive, through acts uncouth 110
Toward making, than repose on aught found made:
So, better, age, exempt
From strife, should know, than tempt
Further. Thou waitedst age: wait death nor be afraid!

Enough now, if the Right 115
And Good and Infinite
Be named here, as thou callest thy hand thine own,
With knowledge absolute,
Subject to no dispute
From fools that crowded youth, nor let thee feel alone. 120

Be there, for once and all,
Severed great minds from small,
Announced to each his station in the Past!
Was I, the world arraigned,
Were they, my soul disdained, 125
Right? Let age speak the truth and give us peace at last!

Now, who shall arbitrate?
Ten men love what I hate,
Shun what I follow, slight what I receive;
Ten, who in ears and eyes   130
Match me: we all surmise,
They this thing, and I that: whom shall my soul believe?

Not on the vulgar mass
Called "work," must sentence pass,
Things done, that took the eye and had the price;   135
O'er which, from level stand,
The low world laid its hand,
Found straightway to its mind, could value in a trice:

But all, the world's coarse thumb
And finger failed to plumb,   140
So passed in making up the main account;
All instincts immature,
All purposes unsure,
That weighed not as his work, yet swelled the man's
        amount:

Thoughts hardly to be packed   145
Into a narrow act,
Fancies that broke through language and escaped;
All I could never be,
All, men ignored in me,
This, I was worth to God, whose wheel the pitcher
        shaped.   150

Ay, note that Potter's wheel,
That metaphor! and feel
Why time spins fast, why passive lies our clay, —

Thou, to whom fools propound,
When the wine makes its round,   155
" Since life fleets, all is change; the Past gone, seize to-
day ! "

Fool! All that is, at all,
Lasts ever, past recall;
Earth changes, but thy soul and God stand sure:
What entered into thee,   160
That was, is, and shall be:
Time's wheel runs back or stops: Potter and clay endure.

He fixed thee, mid this dance
Of plastic circumstance,
This Present, thou, forsooth, wouldst fain arrest: 165
Machinery just meant
To give thy soul its bent,
Try thee and turn thee forth, sufficiently impressed.

What though the earlier grooves
Which ran the laughing loves   170
Around thy base, no longer pause and press?
What thought, about thy rim,
Skull-things in order grim
Grow out, in graver mood, obey the sterner stress?

Look not thou down but up!   175
To uses of a cup,
The festal board, lamp's flash and trumpet's peal,
The new wine's foaming flow,
The Master's lips aglow!
Thou, heaven's consummate cup, what need'st thou with
earth's wheel?   180

But I need, now as then,
Thee, God, who mouldest men;
And since, not even while the whirl was worst,
Did I, — to the wheel of life
With shapes and colours rife,   185
Bound dizzily, — mistake my end, to slake Thy thirst:

So, take and use Thy work:
Amend what flaws may lurk,
What strain o' the stuff, what warpings past the aim!
My times be in Thy hand!   190
Perfect the cup as planned!
Let age approve of youth, and death complete the same!

ONE WORD MORE

I

THERE they are, my fifty men and women
Naming me the fifty poems finished!
Take them, Love, the book and me together:
Where the heart lies, let the brain lie also.

II

Rafael made a century of sonnets,   5
Made and wrote them in a certain volume
Dinted with the silver-pointed pencil
Else he only used to draw Madonnas:
These, the world might view — but one, the volume.
Who that one, you ask? Your heart instructs you.   10
Did she live and love it all her life-time?
Did she drop, his lady of the sonnets,

Die, and let it drop beside her pillow
Where it lay in place of Rafael's glory,
Rafael's cheek so duteous and so loving —   15
Cheek, the world was wont to hail a painter's,
Rafael's cheek, her love had turned a poet's?

III

You and I would rather read that volume,
(Taken to his beating bosom by it)
Lean and list the bosom-beats of Rafael,   20
Would we not? than wonder at Madonnas —
Her, San Sisto names, and Her, Foligno,
Her, that visits Florence in a vision,
Her, that's left with lilies in the Louvre —
Seen by us and all the world in circle.   25

IV

You and I will never read that volume.
Guido Reni, like his own eye's apple
Guarded long the treasure-book and loved it.
Guido Reni dying, all Bologna
Cried, and the world cried too, " Ours, the treasure! "   30
Suddenly, as rare things will, it vanished.

Dante once prepared to paint an angel :
Whom to please? You whisper " Beatrice."
While he mused and traced it and retraced it,
(Peradventure with a pen corroded   35
Still by drops of that hot ink he dipped for,
When, his left hand i' the hair o' the wicked,

Back he held the brow and pricked its stigma,
Bit into the live man's flesh for parchment,
Loosed him, laughed to see the writing rankle,   40
Let the wretch go festering through Florence) —
Dante, who loved well because he hated,
Hated wickedness that hinders loving,
Dante standing, studying his angel, —
In there broke the folk of his Inferno.   45
Says he — " Certain people of importance "
(Such he gave his daily dreadful line to)
" Entered and would seize, forsooth, the poet."
Says the poet — " Then I stopped my painting."

                    VI

You and I would rather see that angel,   50
Painted by the tenderness of Dante,
Would we not? — than read a fresh Inferno.

                   VII

You and I will never see that picture.
While he mused on love and Beatrice,
While he softened o'er his outlined angel,   55
In they broke, those " people of importance:"
We and Bice bear the loss for ever.

                  VIII

What of Rafael's sonnets, Dante's picture?
This: no artist lives and loves, that longs not
Once, and only once, and for one only,   60
(Ah, the prize!) to find his love a language
Fit and fair and simple and sufficient —

Using nature that's an art to others,
Not, this one time, art that's turned his nature.
Ay, of all the artists living, loving, 65
None but would forego his proper dowry, —
Does he paint? he fain would write a poem, —
Does he write? he fain would paint a picture,
Put to proof art alien to the artist's,
Once, and only once, and for one only, 70
So to be the man and leave the artist,
Gain the man's joy, miss the artist's sorrow.

IX

Wherefore?   Heaven's gift takes earth's abatement!
He who smites the rock and spreads the water,
Bidding drink and live a crowd beneath him, 75
Even he, the minute makes immortal,
Proves, perchance, but mortal in the minute,
Desecrates, belike, the deed in doing.
While he smites, how can he but remember,
So he smote before, in such a peril, 80
When they stood and mocked — "Shall smiting help us?"
When they drank and sneered — "A stroke is easy!"
When they wiped their mouths and went their journey,
Throwing him for thanks — "But drought was pleasant."
Thus old memories mar the actual triumph; 85
Thus the doing savours of disrelish;
Thus achievement lacks a gracious somewhat;
O'er-importuned brows becloud the mandate,
Carelessness or consciousness — the gesture.
For he bears an ancient wrong about him, 90
Sees and knows again those phalanxed faces,
Hears, yet one time more, the 'customed prelude —

" How shouldst thou, of all men, smite, and save us?"
Guesses what is like to prove the sequel —
" Egypt's flesh-pots — nay, the drought was better."   95

X

Oh, the crowd must have emphatic warrant
Theirs, the Sinai-forehead's cloven brilliance,
Right arm's rod-sweep, tongue's imperial fiat.
Never dares the man put off the prophet.

XI

Did he love one face from out the thousands,   100
(Were she Jethro's daughter, white and wifely,
Were she but the Æthiopian bondslave,)
He would envy yon dumb patient camel,
Keeping a reserve of scanty water
Meant to save his own life in the desert;   105
Ready in the desert to deliver
(Kneeling down to let his breast be opened)
Hoard and life together for his mistress.

XII

I shall never, in the years remaining,
Paint you pictures, no, nor carve you statues,   110
Make you music that should all-express me;
So it seems: I stand on my attainment.
This of verse alone, one life allows me;
Verse and nothing else have I to give you.
Other heights in other lives, God willing: 115
All the gifts from all the heights, your own, Love!

XIII

Yet a semblance of resource avails us —
Shade so finely touched, love's sense must seize it.
Take these lines, look lovingly and nearly,
Lines I write the first time and the last time.   120
He who works in fresco, steals a hair-brush,
Curbs the liberal hand, subservient proudly,
Cramps his spirit, crowds its all in little,
Makes a strange art of an art familiar,
Fills his lady's missal-marge with flowerets.   125
He who blows through bronze, may breathe through silver,
Fitly serenade a slumbrous princess.
He who writes, may write for once as I do.

XIV

Love, you saw me gather men and women,
Live or dead or fashioned by my fancy,   130
Enter each and all, and use their service,
Speak from every mouth, — the speech, a poem.
Hardly shall I tell my joys and sorrows,
Hopes and fears, belief and disbelieving;
I am mine and yours — the rest be all men's,   135
Karshish, Cleon, Norbert, and the fifty.
Let me speak this once in my true person,
Not as Lippo, Roland, or Andrea,
Though the fruit of speech be just this sentence:
Pray you, look on these my men and women,   140
Take and keep my fifty poems finished;
Where my heart lies, let my brain lie also!
Poor the speech; be how I speak, for all things.

XV

Not but that you know me!   Lo, the moon's self!
Here in London, yonder late in Florence,   145
Still we find her face, the thrice-transfigured.
Curving on a sky imbrued with colour,
Drifted over Fiesole by twilight,
Came she, our new crescent of a hair's-breadth.
Full she flared it, lamping Samminiato,   150
Rounder 'twixt the cypresses and rounder,
Perfect till the nightingales applauded.
Now, a piece of her old self, impoverished,
Hard to greet, she traverses the house-roofs,
Hurries with unhandsome thrift of silver,   155
Goes dispiritedly, glad to finish.

XVI

What, there's nothing in the moon noteworthy?
Nay: for if that moon could love a mortal,
Use, to charm him (so to fit a fancy),
All her magic ('tis the old sweet mythos),   160
She would turn a new side to her mortal,
Side unseen of herdsman, huntsman, steersman —
Blank to Zoroaster on his terrace,
Blind to Galileo on his turret,
Dumb to Homer, dumb to Keats — him, even!   165
Think, the wonder of the moonstruck mortal —
When she turns round, comes again in heaven,
Opens out anew for worse or better!
Proves she like some portent of an iceberg
Swimming full upon the ship it founders,   170
Hungry with huge teeth of splintered crystals?

Proves she as the paved work of a sapphire
Seen by Moses when he climbed the mountain?
Moses, Aaron, Nadab, and Abihu
Climbed and saw the very God, the Highest,   175
Stand upon the paved work of a sapphire.
Like the bodied heaven in his clearness
Shone the stone, the sapphire of that paved work,
When they ate and drank and saw God also!

XVII

What were seen?   None knows, none ever shall know.   180
Only this is sure — the sight were other,
Not the moon's same side, born late in Florence,
Dying now impoverished here in London.
God be thanked, the meanest of his creatures
Boasts two soul-sides, one to face the world with,   185
One to show a woman when he loves her!

XVIII

This I say of me, but think of you, Love!
This to you — yourself my moon of poets!
Ah, but that's the world's side, there's the wonder,
Thus they see you, praise you, think they know you!   190
There, in turn I stand with them and praise you —
Out of my own self, I dare to phrase it.
But the best is when I glide from out them,
Cross a step or two of dubious twilight,
Come out on the other side, the novel   195
Silent silver lights and darks undreamed of,
Where I hush and bless myself with silence.

XIX

Oh, their Rafael of the dear Madonnas,
Oh, their Dante of the dread Inferno,
Wrote one song — and in my brain I sing it,　　　200
Drew one angel — borne, see, on my bosom!

EPILOGUE TO ASOLANDO

At the midnight in the silence of the sleep-time,
　　When you set your fancies free,
Will they pass to where — by death, fools think, im-
　　prisoned —
Low he lies who once so loved you, whom you loved so
　　　　　　　　— Pity me?　　　5

Oh to love so, be so loved, yet so mistaken!
　　What had I on earth to do
With the slothful, with the mawkish, the unmanly?
Like the aimless, helpless, hopeless, did I drivel
　　　　　　　　— Being — who?　　　10

One who never turned his back but marched breast for-
　　ward,
　　Never doubted clouds would break,
Never dreamed, though right were worsted, wrong would
　　triumph,
Held we fall to rise, are baffled to fight better,
　　　　　　　　Sleep to wake.　　　15

No, at noonday in the bustle of man's worktime
　　Greet the unseen with a cheer!
Bid him forward, breast and back as either should be,
" Strive and thrive!" cry " Speed, — fight on, fare ever
　　　　　　　　There as here!"　　　20

NOTES

MY STAR

First published in *Men and Women*, 1855. A love lyric supposed to refer to Mrs. Browning. It is a tribute to the personal element in love, " showing how the soul of the loved one reveals itself fully to the sympathetic insight of the lover alone, who, having this revelation, cares nothing if the choice of others be more distinguished."

4. angled spar : a prism, which has the property of breaking up light into its component parts.

9. dartles : darts, probably a word coined by Browning.

11. They must solace themselves with the Saturn above it : others can study and know the planets, he cares to know only his star.

A FACE

A portrait of a beautiful girl painted in words by a poet who had all the sympathies of an artist. " No poem in the volume of *Dramatis Personæ* is connected with pictorial art, unless it be the few lines entitled *A Face*, lines of which Emily Patmore, the wife of Coventry Patmore, the poet, was the subject, and written, as Browning seldom wrote, for the mere record of beauty. That ' little head of hers ' is transferred to Browning's panel in the manner of an early Tuscan piece of ideal loveliness." (Dowden : Life of Browning.)

3. Tuscan's art : the early Tuscan artists frequently painted portraits upon a background of gold.

9. Burthen : burden, load.

11. lithe : easily bent, limber.

14. Correggio: Antonio Allegri da Correggio, a famous Lombard painter.

MY LAST DUCHESS

First published in *Dramatic Lyrics*, 1842. This is one of the earliest specimens of the " dramatic monologues," a variety of verse which became Browning's favorite form. The poem depicts jealousy which has no love in it. A widowed Duke of Ferrara is showing a portrait of his former wife to the envoy of some nobleman whose daughter he is trying to marry. The remarks of the Duke are intended to convey to the envoy and through him to the lady what he demands in his new wife, — the concentration of her whole being on himself and the utmost devotion to his will. Mr. Arthur Symonds says: " The poem is a subtle study in the jealousy of egoism, not a study so much as a creation ; and it places before us, as if bitten out by the etcher's acid, a typical autocrat of the Renaissance, with his serene self-composure of selfishness, quiet, uncompromising cruelty, and genuine devotion to art." Note that although the verses rhyme the effect is that of blank verse.

The Duke speaks throughout the whole poem.

3. Frà Pandolf: Frà Pandolf and Claus of Innsbruck are imaginary artists.

40. lessoned: note the use of this word as a verb.

47. Will't please you rise: The envoy rises from his seat and he and the Duke start for the stairs.

48. I repeat, etc.: the Duke, in spite of his protestations, is anxious to get a good dowry with his new wife.

53. Nay, we'll go Together down, sir: the acme of courtesy.

SONGS FROM PIPPA PASSES

These three songs are taken from Browning's play, *Pippa Passes*, which describes the course of one day in the life of an Italian girl, Felippa or Pippa. The first song is the pure joy of living. The last two verses of it are frequently quoted.

The second song is the lament of a young page that his lady
is so far above him as to prevent his serving her. The third
is a love song, expressing the patience of a lover.

II. 14. Kate the Queen: Catharine Cornaro, the widow of
James II, King of Cyprus. After the death of her husband,
Catharine abdicated her throne in favor of the Republic
of Venice, which granted her a palace at Asolo. There she
lived a peaceful idyllic life, greatly loved by all, for many
years.

26. jesses: little leather thongs or silk strings fastened on
the legs of hawks in the sport of hawking. The leash by which
the hawk was held was fastened to these thongs. When the
hawk was sent up after a bird the leash was untied, leaving the
jesses on the hawk's legs.

III. 27. tarry: wait for.

28. protracted: slow.

EURYDICE TO ORPHEUS

First published in the Royal Academy Catalogue, 1864;
reprinted in the Selections, 1865. " It represents Orpheus
leading Eurydice away from the infernal regions, but with an
implied variation on the story of her subsequent return to
them. She was restored to Orpheus on the condition of his not
looking at her until they reached the upper world; and, as the
legend goes, the condition proved too hard for him to fulfil.
But the face of Leighton's Eurydice wears an intensity of
longing which seems to challenge the forbidden look, and makes
her responsible for it. The poem thus interprets the expression
and translates it into words." (Mrs. Orr: Handbook to
Browning's Works.)

Eurydice is speaking, just before she is carried back into
Hades.

1. But give them me: But give to me the mouth, the eyes,
the brow.

"THE MOTH'S KISS, FIRST"

These little songs are from the long dramatic poem *In a Gondola*. The woman sings them.

4. pursed: contracted, folded up.

7. ope: poetic form for open.

MEETING AT NIGHT — PARTING AT MORNING

First published in *Dramatic Romances and Lyrics*, 1845. The speaker is a lover who seeks his beloved from whom he has to part at morn. These poems are noteworthy for their fusion of human emotion and natural scenery.

15–16. him: the sun. The lover contrasts the sun's path of gold with his need of returning to the world of men and the work of the day.

"HOW THEY BROUGHT THE GOOD NEWS FROM GHENT TO AIX"

First published in *Dramatic Romances and Lyrics*, 1845. "A rousing good story, of which the key-note is the galloping of hard-pushed horses." This poem was written during Browning's first journey to Italy in 1838. The incident is imaginary. Of the poem Browning says: "I wrote it under the bulwark of a vessel off the African coast, after I had been at sea long enough to appreciate even the fancy of a gallop on the back of a certain good horse 'York' then in my stables at home." Two of the horses falling dead by the way, the good steed Roland is left to reach the goal and save Aix. The distance from Ghent to Aix-la-Chapelle is over ninety miles. Hasselt is about eighty miles from Ghent; Dalhem is in sight of Aix. Looz and Tongres are off the direct route. Note how the meter suggests the galloping of horses.

1. I: the imaginary person who is telling the story.

5. postern: the gate through which they had left the city.

10. pique: the point of the saddle.

13. 'Twas moonset: the ride was made between midnight of one day and sunset of the next.

17. Mecheln: the contracted form of Mechelen, Flemish for Mechlin. The cathedral tower has its set of chimes.

43. roan: a horse of a roan color. Roan is a bay, sorrel, or chestnut color, with some white or gray hairs interspersed.

44. croup: the rump or buttocks of a horse.

49. buff-coat: a thick leather coat.

50. jack-boots: long boots coming above the knee and adding considerably to the weight of the rider.

59. burgesses: magistrates of the town.

INCIDENT OF THE FRENCH CAMP

First published in *Dramatic Lyrics*, 1842. In 1809 Napoleon stormed Ratisbon, a city of Bavaria. The incident narrated in this poem is true, but the hero was a man, not a boy. It illustrates the heroism that Napoleon was able to inspire in his men. An old trooper of Napoleon's is telling the story.

1. Ratisbon: Ratisbon has endured seventeen sieges, the last one being that of Napoleon in 1809.

5. With neck out-thrust: there are a number of pictures of Napoleon in this attitude.

11. Lannes: Jean Lannes, Duke of Montebello, one of Napoleon's marshals.

29. flag-bird: eagle on the standard. **Vans:** wings.

THE LOST LEADER

First published in *Dramatic Romances and Lyrics*, 1845. A lament over the defection of a loved and honored chief. It was suggested by Wordsworth's abandonment of the liberal cause. Browning says of this poem: " I can only answer, with something of shame and contrition, that I undoubtedly had Wordsworth in mind, but simply as a model; you know an artist takes one or two striking traits in the features of his

model and uses them to start his fancy on a flight which may
end far enough from the good man or woman who happened
to be sitting for nose or eye.   I thought of the great Poet's
abandonment of Liberalism at an unlucky juncture, and no
repaying consequence that I could ever see.   But once call
my fancy portrait Wordsworth, and how much more ought
one to say!"   Perhaps we may consider this as a denial.   The
first of the poem can be applied to Wordsworth only remotely,
as Wordsworth, although pensioned, never was decorated
with an order.   Compare Whittier's **Ichabod** in which the poet
records his feelings at what he judged to be a defection of
Daniel Webster from the cause of freedom.

Wordsworth, when a young man, held very liberal or revo-
lutionary views.   After the French Revolution he abandoned
those ideas and became a conservative.   The person speaking
is supposed to be a liberal who is indignant with Wordsworth
because he had deserted the liberal cause.

2. riband: ribbon of a medal or order of nobility.

3. one gift: success.

8. Rags: we could have given him only rags to wear as
a reward for being one of us.   If he had been noble enough to
think our rags as fine apparel as king's garments, he would
have been proud to wear them.

13. Shakespeare was of us: Shakespeare, Milton, Burns,
and Shelley were favorable to the liberal cause while they lived.
Now from their graves they are watching and waiting for the
cause to be successful.   He who might have been numbered
with these great ones alone has fallen away.

19. quiescence: inactivity in the liberal cause.   Deeds
will be done, but not by him.

20. crouch: in the attitude of subjection.

20. whom the rest bade aspire: the allusion is to the efforts
of the liberals to inspire the lower classes to improve their
condition.

28. Never glad confident morning again: even if he should return after his apostasy, we could not have the same confident feeling toward him as before.

LOVE AMONG THE RUINS

First published in *Men and Women*, 1855. In this poem is depicted a pastoral solitude where are buried the remains of an ancient city, fabulous in its magnificence and strength. The speaker is to meet his sweetheart in a ruined turret that marks the spot where the king of the city used to watch the racing chariots as they circled it in their course. He is absorbed in a melancholy contemplation of the transitoriness of human glory. Against this fleeting background stands out clearly the only thing that is eternal, which is Love.

No historical city is meant, but Browning may have had in mind the Homeric Thebes or perhaps Babylon, certainly not Rome, as some have suggested.

The metrical form of the poem is unusual. Note how the short even-numbered verses serve as echoes for the verses preceding.

5. Tinkle: notice the suggestiveness of this word. It pictures the tinkling of the sheep bells as the sheep move slowly homeward, stopping and feeding on the way.

39. caper: a low shrub growing on old walls in fissures of rocks in the countries bordering the Mediterranean.

40. Overscored: crossed back and forth.

47. minions: courtiers.

51. folding: shutting up in the folds. **many-tinkling fleece**: the fleece is used here for the sheep with their bells.

57. caught soul: became filled with a desire to reach the goal.

65. causeys: causeways.

HOME-THOUGHTS, FROM ABROAD

First published in *Dramatic Romances and Lyrics*, 1845. A loving reminiscence of an English April and May by one who is living in Italy and whose heart is yearning for the delights

of spring in his native England.   Appreciation is heightened
by contrast, the buttercup being pronounced far brighter than
the " gaudy melon-flower" which the exiled Englishman has
at this moment before him.   This is one of the few poems in
which Browning uses the scenery of his own country.

    6. bole: the body or trunk of a tree.

    14. he sings each song twice over: an instance of Brown-
ing's keen observation of the phenomena of nature.

    19. the little children's dower: the buttercups are nature's
free gift to children.

HOME–THOUGHTS, FROM THE SEA

    First published in *Dramatic Romances and Lyrics,* 1845.
An utterance of patriotic pride aroused by the sight of Tra-
falgar.   One of the few poems in which Browning shows his
English patriotism.

    1. Cape Saint Vincent: the southwestern point of Portugal,
the scene of Nelson's brilliant victory over the Spanish, 1797.

    2. Cadiz Bay: on the southeastern coast of Spain.   An
English fleet overcame a Spanish fleet there in 1596.

    3. Trafalgar: here Nelson won his great victory, October 21,
1805, over the French fleet, — the victory which freed England
from the menace of invasion by Napoleon.

    7. Jove's planet: the planet Jupiter.

THE ITALIAN IN ENGLAND

    First published in *Dramatic Romances and Lyrics,* 1845.   In
1844 Browning visited Italy and wrote this poem.   It does
not represent any definite historical incident, but such as
might have occurred in the life of some Italian patriot who had
fled from Italy and was now an exile living in England.   As
the patriot reflects upon the incidents of his escape and flight
from Italy, the wish comes to him that he may see the dis-
comfiture of his enemies and that he may revisit Italy and see

once more the woman who had aided him to escape even at the risk of her own life.

3. Austria: at the Congress of Vienna in 1815 Austria was given Lombardy and Venetia. Although most of the inhabitants submitted to the foreign rule, there were always small bands of patriots who endeavored to throw off the Austrian yoke and to make Italy independent. Both Browning and Mrs. Browning were in sympathy with these efforts, and both have frequent allusions to the liberation of Italy in their works.

8. Charles: Charles Albert, Prince of Carignano, of the younger branch of the house of Savoy. As indicated in the poem, in his youth he was in sympathy with liberal principles, but later left his friends in the lurch and went over to the Austrian side.

19. Metternich: a famous Austrian diplomat, an enemy of Italian freedom. **friend**: sarcastic.

20. Charles's miserable end: see note on Charles, line 8.

41. crypt: hiding place.

75. duomo: the famous cathedral of St. Anthony at Padua.

76. Tenebræ: darkness. The service commemorative of the Crucifixion, in which fifteen lighted candles are put out one at a time, symbolizing the growing darkness of the world up to the time of the Crucifixion.

82. From Christ and Freedom: the watchword agreed upon between the Patriot and his friends.

111. How very long, etc.: " How very long is it since I have thought of aught else beside the good of Italy!"

116. Charles: see note on Charles, line 8.

127. Under his new employers: the government of Austria.

161. So much for idle wishing: note how this gives a realistic touch to the poem.

UP AT A VILLA — DOWN IN THE CITY

First published in *Men and Women*, 1855. A view of life as seen by an Italian of quality who does not care for country life but who is too poor to live in the city. It is a lively description of the amusing things of city life as contrasted with the dulness of life in a villa.

4. by Bacchus: "Per Baccho" — Italians still swear by the wine-god.

13. awry: out of line.

27. foam-bows: miniature rainbows.

28. pash: strike violently, dash.

29. conch: shell.

33. corn: any small grain, but not the maize of America.

34. thrid: thread.

35. cicala: the cricket, whose note stuns the ear.

39. diligence: mail coach.

42. Pulcinello-trumpet: the trumpet announcing the beginning of the Punch and Judy show.

43. scene-picture: formerly in Italian towns it was customary to post in some conspicuous place, as at the post-office, copies of decrees, censure of the clergy, edicts of the local lord, poems, notices of sermons, and other matters of general interest.

44. liberal thieves: the party striving for Italian independence.

47. flowery marge: the margin decorated with floral designs.

48. Dante: Dante Alighieri, 1265–1321, the most celebrated Italian poet.

Boccaccio: Giovanni Boccaccio, 1313–1375, a celebrated Italian novelist and poet.

Petrarca: Francesco Petrarca, or Petrarch, 1304–1374, one of the most famous of Italian poets and scholars. He is famous for his sonnets.

Saint Jerome: a famous father of the Latin Church, 340–420. He published the Latin version of the Bible known as the Vulgate.

Cicero: Marcus Tullius Cicero, 106 B.C.–43 B.C., the most celebrated orator, philosopher, and statesman of Rome.

51. our Lady: the Virgin Mary, the seven swords symbolizing her sorrows and contrasting naïvely with the pink gauze and spangles.

56. tax upon salt: a reference to the taxes imposed on all provisions coming into the city.

THE PIED PIPER OF HAMELIN

First published in *Dramatic Lyrics*, 1842. This poem was written to amuse little Willie Macready, the son of Macready, the actor. It is based on one of the numerous legends that deal with the subject of cheating magicians of a promised reward for service rendered, and of the revenge they take. According to Verstegan, " A piper named Bunting undertook for a certain sum of money to free the town of Hamelin, in Brunswick, of the rats which infested it; but when he had drowned all the rats in the river Weser, the townsmen refused to pay the sum agreed upon. The piper, in revenge, collected the children of Hamelin, and enticed them by his piping into a cavern in the side of the mountain Koppenberg, which instantly closed upon them."

This poem is an allegory the meaning of which is given in Stanza XV.

For a beautiful dramatic treatment of this theme, see Mrs. Josephine Preston Peabody's *The Piper*.

Browning's poem is chiefly remarkable for its rollicking wealth of rhymes.

15. sprats: a small fish often confused with herring.

23. noddy: simpleton, fool.

25. gowns lined with ermine: in Europe civic officers formerly were furnished with gorgeous uniforms including robes lined or trimmed with ermine. These they wore whenever they appeared in public.

26. dolts: blockheads.

50. paunch: stomach.

68. Trump of Doom's: the sound of the angel Gabriel's horn which is to arouse the dead.

87. old-fangled: old-fashioned.

89. Cham: usually Khan, the title of the ruler of the Tartar Empire.

91. Nizam: the title of the sovereign of Hyderabad in India.

123. Julius Cæsar: Shakespeare's *Julius Cæsar*, Act I, Scene 2.

136. psaltery: a musical instrument of the zither group, having many strings which are plucked with the fingers.

138. dry saltery: a place for curing meat or fish by drying and salting.

139. nuncheon: luncheon.

141. puncheon: barrel.

153. perked: to perk is to toss up the head with affected smartness.

169. poke: pouch or pocket.

177. Bagdat: Bagdad. **prime:** the choice portion; compare, prime ribs of beef.

182. bate: lower the amount, reduct; compare, rebate. **stiver:** a small Dutch coin.

188. piebald: party-colored, alluding to the dress of the Piper.

260. needle's eye: Matthew XIX, 24, "It is easier for a camel to go through the eye of a needle, than for a rich man to enter into the kingdom of God."

296. trepanned: usually written trapanned, ensnared.

"DE GUSTIBUS —"

First published in *Men and Women*, 1855. The expression is *De gustibus non disputandum*, "there is no accounting for tastes." In exquisite contrast Browning sets his two loves, England and Italy. There is a suggestion of the long struggle of Italy for freedom at the close of the poem.

2. our loves remain: if after death we love the same things we loved in life.

4. cornfield: a field of grain with poppies fluttering in it.

11. bean-flowers' boon: the delicious scent of a field of beans in blossom.

15. precipice-encurled: surrounded by precipices.

22. cicala: the cricket.

35. the king: another allusion to the efforts of the Italian patriots to free their country from foreign dominion.

36. liver-wing: the right wing under which the liver was placed when the bird was roasted. Here it is used for the right arm.

40. Queen Mary's saying: Mary Tudor grieved so for the loss of Calais in 1588 that she said the word would be found written on her heart.

MEMORABILIA

First published in *Men and Women*, 1855. *Memorabilia* renders homage to Shelley by signalizing the moment when an unappreciative person's remembrance of him was made known, like a moor blank of interest save for the space where the sign of an eagle's flight was found and prized. Professor Corson thinks that the eagle feather "causes an isolated flash of association with the poet of atmosphere, the winds, and the clouds."

INSTANS TYRANNUS

First published in *Men and Women*, 1855. *Instans Tyrannus* is a phrase taken from a well-known ode of Horace, meaning "Threatening tyrant." The poem supposes that for some unknown reason a poor, contemptible man was the object of the tyrant's hate. The tyrant becomes exasperated by the very insignificance of the creature: he struck him, tried to bribe him, tempted his flesh and blood. But at the critical moment, the victim threw himself on the protection of God. The wretch

> " caught at God's skirts and prayed!
> So, *I* was afraid!"

It shows how strong the weakest man may become when he is in the right and has the force of good on his side.

15. So, I set my five wits on the stretch: *i.e.* I tried every means to tempt him, to bribe him, to harm him through his friends or relatives, but in vain. He was so obscure that he could not be harmed by any of these means.

18. perdue: hidden.

21. cates: dainties.   **spilth**: that which is spilled; here the wine.

29. pelf: booty; compare, to pilfer.

31. chafe: impatience.

33. nit: the egg of some minute insect.

35. humor: idea.

44. gravamen: grievance.

63. marge: margin, edge.

64. targe: shield.

65. boss: the stud on the center of a shield.

TRAY

First published in *Dramatic Idyls*, 1879. The writer of the poem is urging three bards to tell him a tale of a hero with a soul. The first bard begins a tale of a knight, but is soon stopped. The second bard begins a blood-curdling tale, but also fails to satisfy the hearer and is stopped likewise. Then the third bard begins a good story of the dog Tray, the real theme of the poem. The last touch in this praise of Tray is the picture of the unconscious inferiority of one of the bystanders, who so little appreciates the spiritual quality of heroism that he proposes to vivisect the dog's brain and locate his valor. The incident of the dog was actually witnessed by a friend of Browning's in Paris.

4. helm: helmet.   **eke**: also, in addition.   **habergeon**: a coat of linked mail covering the neck and breast.

7. ope: poetic form for open.

19. instinctive dog: *i.e.* an animal which acts on instinct.

HERVÉ RIEL

Published in *Pacchiarotto*, 1876. This stirring ballad was first published in The Cornhill Magazine in 1871 and the proceeds, one hundred pounds sterling, were given to the fund for the sufferers from the siege of Paris. The poem is a gracious tribute from an Englishman to the French, and shows how a Frenchman can do a great service to his country and ask but an insignificant reward. The story is historical. In the war between the English and Dutch and the French, after the battle of La Hogue, 1692, the French fleet was in danger of capture by the English. A simple Breton sailor guided the fleet through a channel which the pilots declared impassable and thus saved it from capture by the English. In the official account the sailor is said to have asked for dismissal from the service as his reward. Browning, however, made the story more dramatic by contrasting the greatness of the achievement and the slightness of the reward the sailor asked for and received.

4. Like a crowd of frightened porpoises (which) a shoal of sharks pursue.

5. Saint-Malo: a seaport at the mouth of the Rance.

8. Damfreville: the commander of the French squadron which was fleeing.

17. starboard: right side. **port**: left side.

21. with flow at full beside: even when the tide is high.

30. Plymouth Sound: an English naval station.

43. pressed: see note on pressing, *Marching Along*, line 3. **Tourville**: the French admiral.

44. Croisickese: a native of Croisic, a small town in Brittany.

46. Malouins: inhabitants of Saint-Malo.

49. Grève: the sands between Saint-Malo and Mount Saint Michel. **disembogues**: empties.

50. Is it love the lying's for? *i.e.* Do you lie for the mere love of it?

61. Solidor: at the mouth of the Rance.

82. hollas: calls, cries out, shouts.

128. a head in white and black: a figurehead on a ship.

131. bore the bell: gained the victory.

134. Louvre: the Palace of the Louvre in Paris is the great national gallery where are gathered statues or portraits of the great men of France. There one searches in vain for a statue of Hervé Riel.

PHEIDIPPIDES

First published in *Dramatic Idyls*, 1879.

Χαίρετε, νικῶμεν. Rejoice; we conquer.

The facts related in this poem belong to Greek legendary history, and are told by Herodotus and other writers. "When Athens was threatened by the invading Persians, she sent a running messenger to Sparta, to demand help against the foreign foe. The mission was unsuccessful. But the 'runner' Pheidippides fell in on his return with the god Pan; and though alone among the Greeks the Athenians had refused to honor him, Pan promised to fight with them in the coming battle. Pheidippides was present, when this battle — that of Marathon — was fought and won. He 'ran' once more, to announce the victory at Athens; and fell, dead, with the words 'Rejoice; we conquer!' on his lips." (Handbook to Browning's Works.)

2. dæmons: tutelary divinities, between men and gods.

4. Her of the ægis and spear: Pallas Athena. The ægis was a shield having on it the head of the Gorgon Medusa, and was worn by Pallas Athena.

5. ye of the bow and the buskin: Diana, the huntress, whose statues often represent her as wearing the buskin or high hunting boot.

8. Pan: the god of the forest. He was represented as half man and half goat and his appearance caused people to be frightened; hence from the name of the god comes the word

" panic." The belief was that Pan turned the tide of battle at Marathon by filling the enemy with terror.

9. Archons: the chief magistrates of Athens were called archons, rulers. **tettix:** the grasshopper. " The Athenians sometimes wore golden grasshoppers in their hair as badges of honor, because these insects are supposed to spring from the ground, and thus they showed that they were sprung from the original inhabitants of the country." (Berdoe: Browning Cyclopædia.)

12. reach Sparta: in the southernmost part of Greece, about 140 miles from Athens.

13. Persia has come: Darius the Great, at the head of an immense Persian force, invaded Greece, 483 B.C., but was defeated in the battle of Marathon.

18. water and earth: Darius sent heralds into all parts of Greece to require, according to the custom of the Persians when they wished to exact submission, water and earth, as these two elements were the symbols of freedom.

19. Eretria: a city on the island of Eubœa, north of Athens.

31. quarry: prey.

32. Phoibus: Phœbus Apollo.

38. the moon, half-orbed: " The Spartans wished to help the Athenians, but were unable to give them any present succor, as they did not like to break their established law. It was the ninth day of the first decade, and they could not march out of Sparta on the ninth, when the moon had not reached the full. So they waited for the full of the moon." Herodotus.

41. except for that sparkle: were it not for the fervor which the name of Athens inspires, I would have burnt up with the rage that was in me.

47. filleted victim: the head of a victim for sacrifice was decorated with ribbons. **fulsome libation:** a libation was an offering of oil or wine poured on the ground in honor of some god. **fulsome:** lavish, copious, abundant.

49. Oak and olive and bay: the leaves of the oak, olive, and bay or laurel were used for making wreaths or crowns, the marks of honor.

52. Parnes: Herodotus calls the mountain Parthenion.

62. Erebos: Hades.

65. majestical Pan: " Pan was the protecting deity of flocks and herds and hunters. He was represented by the ancients with a pug nose, very hairy, and with horns and feet of a goat. He was described as wandering about in the woods and dales and hills, playing with the nymphs and looking after the flocks. . . . He was the god of prophecy, and there were oracles of Pan." (Berdoe: Browning Cyclopædia.) Read Mrs. Browning's poem *The Dead Pan*.

72. Athens . . . holds me aloof: up to this time Athens had refused to give Pan the usual honors of worship.

73. fane: shrine, altar.

80. Goat-thigh to greaved-thigh: Pan with his thighs of a goat would fight side by side with the Athenians whose thighs were protected by leg armor or greaves.

83. Fennel . . . whatever it bode: what it meant was that the great battle was to be fought in a fennel field, Marathon, as fennel in Greek is Marathon.

87. we stand no more on the razor's edge: a Greek proverbial expression for extreme peril.

88. guerdon: prize.

89. Miltiades: one of the ten Athenian generals commanding the army that won the battle.

96. pelf: see note on *Instans Tyrannus*, line 29.

106. Akropolis: the citadel of a Greek city was called Akropolis.

107. meed: reward.

THE PATRIOT

First published in *Men and Women*, 1855. " An old story," because in all ages men have experienced this fickleness of popular favor. Only a year ago, the " patriot" entered the

city a hero, amid the shouts of the people. To-day he passes
out of it on his way to execution. He is " safer so," he thinks,
for the reward men have withheld awaits him at the hands of
God. Perhaps Browning caught a hint for this poem from
his life in Florence, where Italian patriots were trying to
liberate their country.

12. To give it (to) my loving friends to keep.

17. set: placed there by their friends as they could not go
to the place of execution on account of their crippled condition. In this stanza Browning gives a picture of the people
formerly wild with enthusiasm over the " patriot," but now
all crowding to get the best places to see him executed.

RABBI BEN EZRA

First published in *Dramatis Personæ*, 1864. Rabbi Ben
Ezra, or Ibn Ezra, was a learned Jew of the eleventh century.
He was poor, but studied hard and wrote many treatises on
Hebrew grammar, astronomy, mathematics, and commen-
taries on the books of the Bible. " The most striking feature
of Rabbi Ben Ezra's philosophy is his estimate of age. According to him the soul is eternal, but it completes the first stage
of its experience in the earthly life; and the climax of the
earthly life is attained, not in the middle of it, but at its close.
Age is therefore a period, not only of rest, but of fruition."
(Handbook to Browning's Works.)

So far as we can judge from the remains of the old Jewish
rabbi's works, Browning has faithfully represented his
philosophy. The aged rabbi is addressing some young friend.
He says that we should not remonstrate with the hopes and
aspirations of youth, but should encourage them. Satis-
faction with mere material things is a sign of the brute. Yet
we must not despise the flesh, for the highest achievement is
where the flesh and spirit work in harmony. Keeping this
always before us we shall be ready for age, in the summing
up of life's gains and losses. All imperfect plans, the half-

achieved deeds, the things dreamed of but not dared — these are to count with God. In death comes the fruition of all youth and the consummation of age. Compare with this thought Tennyson's *St. Simeon Stylites* for an account of a lower form of ascetic ideal.

7. Not that, amassing flowers, etc.: I do not remonstrate that youth, amassing flowers, sighed " Which rose make ours, which lily leave, and then change my choice?"

24. Irks care: does care irk . . . does doubt fret.

29. Nearer we hold of God: have title to a nearer relationship with God.

37. paradox: a statement that is apparently contradictory.

40. What I aspired to be: " 'tis not what man does which exalts him but what man would do." *Saul*, 296.

47. Thy body at its best: how far can the body help the soul on its lone way.

50. Past: the past of his own life.

52. dole: part, share.

57. I, who saw power, see now Love perfect too: in my youth I saw God as power only; now I see him as love also.

68. Spite of this flesh to-day: the old idea of the flesh as something we must subdue.

75. term: end, limit.

77. for aye: for ever.

84. indue: put on.

87. Leave the fire ashes: " fire" is the conflicts of life, " gold" is whatever has proved to be of permanent worth, while " ashes" is used for whatever has failed to stand the test of time.

92. A certain moment: the moment between the fading of the sunset and the coming of the darkness of night. This is the time to appraise the work of the day. So old age is the period for appraising the life of the past.

105. To act to-morrow what he learns to-day: to put into action to-morrow what he has learned to-day.

109. As it was better, etc.: youth should not be content with what has been gained, but should ever strive upward toward something better, even if its work is crude.

124. Was I, the world arraigned: the relative pronouns are omitted. "Was I (whom) the world arraigned or were they (whom) my soul disdained, right?"

135. that took the eye and had the price: cheap, tawdry things that easily measure up to the world's low standard.

138. trice: an instant of time.

150. whose wheel the pitcher shaped: the metaphor of the potter's wheel is quite common. Compare Is. 64, 8, "But now, O Lord, thou art our father; we are the clay and thou art our potter, and we all are the work of thy hand." Compare also Edward Fitzgerald's *Rubaiyat of Omar Khayyam*, stanzas 83–90.

169. What though the earlier grooves, etc.: as the pitcher grows in the hands of the potter, no longer the tools press laughing loves, symbolical of youth, in the clay, but graver objects, symbolical of age, take their place as the potter finishes the rim.

ONE WORD MORE

(To E. B. B. [Elizabeth Barrett Browning], 1855.)

This poem, originally an epilogue to the collection of poems called *Men and Women*, fifty in number, was the dedication of the poet to his wife. This volume was in a sense a return to her for her *Sonnets from the Portuguese*, in which she poured out her love for him, and in this poem in a happy manner he expresses his love for her, his " moon of poets."

" The meanest of God's creatures

' Boasts two soul-sides, one to face the world with,
One to show a woman when he loves her ! '

The poor workman, the most unskilful artisan, will strive to do something which shall express his utmost effort, to present

to his love, and the greatest geniuses of the world have been
actuated by a similar motive.   Raphael, not content with painting, must pour out his soul in poetry for the woman of his heart.
. . . Dante even proposed to paint for Beatrice (his love) an
angel — traced it perchance with the corroded pen with which
he pricked the stigma in the brow of the wicked. . . .   No
artist lives and loves who desires not for once and for one to express himself in a language natural to him and the occasion,
but which to others is but an art ; and so the painter will forgo
his painting and write a poem, the writer will try to paint a
picture ' once and for one only ' —

> ' So to be the man and leave the artist.'

"Why is this?   When a man comes before the world as leader,
teacher, prophet, artist, or poet, in any capacity which is his
proper business, he is open to the unsympathetic criticism of a
world which is ever exacting and always ungrateful in exact
proportion to the magnitude of the work done for it.   Under
these circumstances the real stuff in the man seldom appears ;
when, however, he presents himself before the sympathetic
soul of the woman who loves him, he no longer works for the
critic, no longer acts a part, no longer appears in a character
distasteful to himself. . . .   But the poet says he shall never
paint pictures, carve statues, nor express himself in music : for
his wife he stands on his power of verse alone, and so he bids her
take the lines of this love poem, which he has written for her.
. . . He will speak to her not dramatically, as he spoke in the
poems in his book, but in his own true person.   She knows him
under both aspects, as the moon of Florence is the same which
shines in London, though she has put off her Italian glory, and
hurries dispiritedly through the gloomy skies of England.   Could
the moon really love a mortal, she has a side she could turn
towards him, unseen as yet by herdsman, or astronomer on his
turret.   Dumb to Homer, to Keats even, she would speak to
him.   And so the poet has for his love

' A side the world has never seen,'

the novel

' Silent silver lights and darks undreamed of.' "

(Berdoe: Browning Cyclopædia.)

5. Rafael: Raphael Sanzio, 1483-1520, a celebrated Italian painter. Browning prefers the Italian form of the name. **century of sonnets:** there is no evidence that Raphael wrote more than three or four sonnets.

7. Dinted: written.

10. Who that one: the lady to whom Raphael is said to have written was Margherita (La Fornarina), the baker's daughter, whose likeness appears in several of his most famous pictures.

20. list: listen to, hear.

22. Her, San Sisto names: in line 22 and the three following lines Browning names the four most famous Madonnas of Raphael, — the Madonna di San Sisto (the " Sistine Madonna "), now in the Dresden gallery; the Madonna di Foligno, now in the Vatican; the Madonna at Florence (" Madonna del Granduca "), which represents her " as appearing to a votary in a vision," now in the Pitti Palace, Florence; and the " Madonna of the Garden" (" La Belle Jardinière "), at the Louvre.

27. Guido Reni: a celebrated painter of the Bolognese school, 1575-1642. This book does not seem to have been a book of sonnets, but a volume of a hundred designs drawn by Raphael.

32. Dante: Dante Alighieri, the most celebrated Italian poet, was master of all the science of his time. He was a skilful draftsman, and tells us that on the anniversary of the death of Beatrice, he drew an angel on a tablet.

33. Beatrice: Beatrice Portinari, 1266-1290, an Italian lady loved by Dante.

35. Peradventure with a pen corroded: when Dante tried to draw an angel for Beatrice, perhaps he found the pen spoiled

for such work of love, corroded by the bitter scorn with which
he had written about evil men.

37. his left hand i' the hair o' the wicked: in the Inferno,
Cantos 32, 33. In this manner he compels a reluctant soul to
speak.

41. Let the wretch go festering through Florence: most of
the men to whom Dante refers in the Inferno were dead, but one
or two were still living when he wrote.

44. Dante standing: Dante says in his *Vita Nuova*, Chapter
XXXV, that a year after Beatrice's death he was drawing an
angel when certain people of importance came in to see him,
and after they were gone the idea of writing a poem to Beatrice
came to him.

57. Bice: a shortened form for Beatrice.

63. Using nature that's an art to others: every artist, when
he loves so greatly as Browning, wishes to express himself in
a medium that is not naturally his, but which his impassioned
state inspires him to. Thus a painter will write a sonnet; a
poet, paint a picture.

71. So to be the man and leave the artist: for this one time
the artist wants to be himself and not an artist, and to express
himself as other men do and not as an artist.

73. Heaven's gift takes earth's abatement: "The artist's
sorrow as contrasted with the man's joy is illustrated from the
experience of Moses in conducting the children of Israel out of
Egypt. (Exodus, Ch. XVII.) His achievement savors of
dis-relish because of the grumbling unbelief of the people, and
because of the ungracious irritation into which he has been be-
trayed even when taxing his God-given power to the utmost in
their behalf. He must hold steadily to his majesty as a prophet
or he cannot control and so serve the crowd, but he covets the
man's joy of doing service to the woman whom he loves."

101. Jethro's daughter: Zipporah, the wife of Moses.

102. Æthiopian bondslave: an Æthiopian slave whom Moses
took to wife, Numbers, Ch. XII, 1.

103. He would envy: the man does not dare put off his prophetic powers, the artist put off his art before the world. But if he loves a woman enough, he would gladly do it, even though it means death.

120. Lines I write the first time and the last time: this is the first time Browning has written in his own character to express his own emotions.

121. He who works in fresco: the fresco painter uses large brushes and large free strokes. Now he takes a fine brush and paints like a miniaturist or an illuminator.

125. missal-marge: the border of the missal or prayer book.

126. who blows through bronze: he who is used to blow a martial strain on a trumpet will play a soft serenade on a silver flute.

129. you saw me gather men and women: Browning usually writes dramatically, giving the experiences and uttering the words of the characters he had created.

136. Karshish . . . Andrea: these are characters which appear in the poems that make up the book, *Men and Women*.

147. Curving on a sky imbrued with colour: " In Florence they had seen the new moon, a mere crescent over the hill Fiesole, and had watched its growth till it hung, round and full, over the church of San Miniato. Now, in London, the moon is in its last quarter."

155. with unhandsome thrift of silver: her silver grows less, as she wanes.

160. mythos: the Greek word from which comes myth. According to the Greek myth, Diana, the moon goddess, fell in love with a beautiful young shepherd, Endymion. Nightly she used to visit him while he slept.

163. Zoroaster: the founder of the Irano-Persian religion, of which the chief god was Varuna, the god of light. Zoroaster studied the stars and from their positions foretold the future.

164. Galileo: a celebrated Italian astronomer, 1564-1642.

165. Dumb to Homer: Homer wrote a poem in praise of the

moon-goddess Diana. **Keats:** John Keats was the author of the poem *Endymion* based on the myth of the love of Diana and the shepherd Endymion.

172. the paved work of sapphire: Exodus, Ch. XXIV, 9, 10. " Then went up Moses, and Aaron, Nadab, and Abihu, and seventy of the elders of Israel: And they saw the God of Israel: and there was under his feet as it were a paved work of a sapphire stone, and as it were the body of heaven in his clearness."

EPILOGUE TO ASOLANDO

The last poem that Browning wrote, his ultimate expression of his noble optimism. " One evening just before his death illness, the poet was reading this from a proof to his daughter-in-law and his sister. He said: ' It almost looks like bragging to say this, and as if I ought to cancel it; but it's the simple truth; and as it's true, it shall stand.' " Compare Tennyson's *Crossing the Bar.*

INDEX OF TITLES

The references are to pages.   The first reference is to the text; the
second, to the notes.